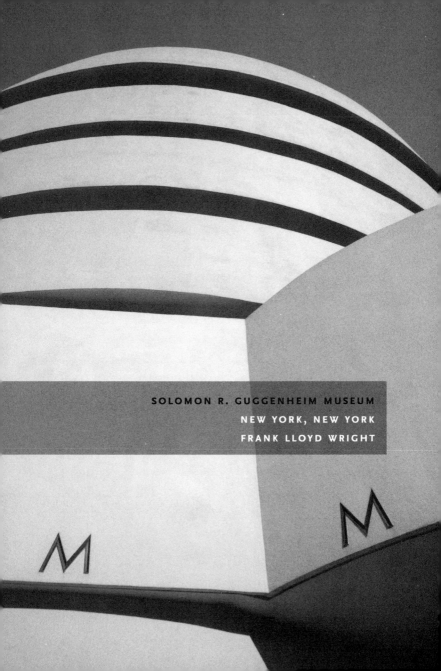

SOLOMON R. GUGGENHEIM MUSEUM

NEW YORK, NEW YORK

FRANK LLOYD WRIGHT

WRITING ARCHITECTURE

A Practical Guide

to Clear Communication

about the Built Environment

CARTER WISEMAN

TRINITY UNIVERSITY PRESS   ♦   *San Antonio*

The author gratefully acknowledges the support of Furthermore, a program of the J.M. Kaplan Fund.

Published by Trinity University Press
San Antonio, Texas 78212

Trinity University Press strives to produce its books using methods and materials in an environmentally sensitive manner. We favor working with manufacturers that practice sustainable management of all natural resources, produce paper using recycled stock, and manage forests with the best possible practices for people, biodiversity, and sustainability. The press is a member of the Green Press Initiative, a nonprofit program dedicated to supporting publishers in their efforts to reduce their impacts on endangered forests, climate change, and forest-dependent communities.

The paper used in this publication meets the minimum requirements of the American National Standard for Information Sciences—Permanence of Paper for Printed Library Materials, ANSI 39.48-1992.

Cover design by Jamie Stolarski
Book design by BookMatters, Berkeley

Photo credits: p. ii: Solomon R. Guggenheim Museum, © iStockphoto/ jpfigueiredo; p. 10–11: Chapel of Notre Dame du Haut, © Shutterstock/Alex Justus; p. 43: Seagram Building, © Foto Sotto; p. 69: courtesy of the American Historic Buildings Survey; p. 121: Rockefeller Center, © iStockphoto/Michael Denijs; p. 149: Brunelleschi's Dome, © Shutterstock/Santi Rodriguez; p. 167: Guggenheim Museum Bilbao, © iStockphoto/borjalaria; p. 187: Phillips Exeter Academy Library, © Jonathan Reike; p. 204–205: Louvre Pyramid, © iStockphoto/Ristoo; p. 215: Bauhaus Building, © iStockphoto/typo-graphics; p. 221: Yale Art and Architecture Building, © Shutterstock/Ritu Manoj Jethani; p. 229 (author photo): Owen Wiseman.

ISBN 978-1-59534-149-5 paper
ISBN 978-1-59534-150-1 ebook

CIP data on file at the Library of Congress

18   17   16   15   14 | 5   4   3   2   1

To my family,

my students, and

my teachers

CONTENTS

INTRODUCTION

Anyone who produces, promotes, or teaches architecture must depend on accurate analysis and lucid explication to encourage design that may make the world a better place. Every successful work of architecture is centered on a core idea. Writing on architecture should be inseparable from the design process itself.

INTRODUCTION

SOME YEARS AGO, a writer for the *Chronicle of Higher Education* declared, "Too many architecture students can't write."[1] Those students have since gone on to become practitioners, and their inability to write is likely to have had seriously negative professional consequences. Robert Campbell, a Pulitzer Prize–winning architecture critic for the *Boston Globe*, condemned in *Architectural Record* much of what even the most prominent practicing architects write as "pretentious illiteracy." He went on to attack their coded language as "Archi-Speak" and warned that "sooner or later, architects (and planners and landscapers and urban designers) must convince someone to hire them or at least bless them with a grant. . . . Nobody is going to trust a dollar to a pompous twit."[2]

Little has changed in the years since Campbell issued his indictment. Having taught courses called "Writing on Architecture" and "Case Studies in Architectural Criticism" for many years at the Yale School of Architecture, I can confirm the claims of both the *Chronicle* and the *Record*. The passage of time does not seem to have improved matters. The decline in the quality of architectural writing is happening at the very moment when the demand for it is increasing, as technology and construction grow more complex. Whether the culprit is the computer, the Internet, texting, or school curricula is open to debate, but clear written communication among even the best-educated people is increasingly rare. For years, surveys have documented a steady decline in the writing skills of American students. But the situation seems especially worrisome in the field of architecture. Murky specifications about, for instance, the environmental impact of a new building can have toxic results; ambiguity about the load-bearing capacity of a structural beam can have fatal implications. Partners in several of the country's leading architecture firms have confessed that they spend only a fraction of their time designing; much of the rest is spent rewriting or correcting what the staff has written. One of these architects, a veteran practitioner and dean of one of the nation's leading architecture schools, put it bluntly: "Architects who can't write are professional toast!"[3]

Why does good writing matter to architecture? Good writing matters regardless of profession, whether it is law, medicine, business, or aerospace. But architecture in particular permeates our lives at every moment and in every dimension. Unlike the other arts—painting, sculpture, music, or theater—architecture is not a matter of choice in our lives, something we decide to take or leave as time and spirit move us. Architecture determines the shape of the places where we live, where we work, where we worship, and where we take our ease. At its most powerful—at the pyramids of Egypt, the Parthenon, Japan's Himeji Castle, St. Peter's in Rome, the Taj Mahal, or the Seagram Building—it ennobles our existence and conveys our highest values across time. For that reason, it is the most comprehensive and complex of the arts. Anyone who makes, produces, promotes, or teaches architecture must depend on accurate analysis and lucid explication to encourage design that may make the world a better place.

There are scores of books on writing. The most useful in my view are the durable small classic *The Elements of Style,* by William Strunk Jr. and E. B. White, and *On Writing Well,* by William Zinsser, both of which address the fundamentals of the craft with efficiency, grace, and wit. This book attempts to address those skills as applied to architecture: by encouraging not just competence, but also enjoyment, and even inspiration.

For the student and the practitioner, writing on architecture should be inseparable from the design process itself. Every successful work of architecture is centered on a core idea. Think of Frank Lloyd Wright's 1959 Guggenheim Museum in New York City. Like it or not (architects do, painters never have), Wright's idea was to display works of art in a continuous space that did away with the segmentation of conventional galleries. Or take Le Corbusier's 1955 Chapel of Notre Dame du Haut in Ronchamp, France. There, the idea was to create an uplifting experience through a combination of forms and spaces that would evoke the aspirations and mysteries of spirituality. A less famous example is the library by the Late Modernist architect Louis Kahn at the Phillips Exeter Academy in Exeter, New Hampshire, finished in 1971. What appears at first glance to be a stolid New England brick box is transformed on the interior into a warren of active study spaces centered on an atrium that encourages the users to witness the scholarly activity to which the building is dedicated. These examples come only from relatively recent architectural history. When we travel, we mark our journeys with stops at the cathedrals of France, the temples of Japan and Central America, and the palaces of the Asian subcontinent. Why? Because these buildings are eloquent tributes to the cultures that produced them, and they inform our own.

In each case, the success of the architecture derives from the focus on what the building is for. That goes well beyond the program—the client's description of the building's basic function. For design students, analyzing good—and especially great—buildings in detail and writing about them is an invaluable way to understand the fundamentals of architecture, and later to marshal that analysis into built form.

For practicing architects, expressing the goals of their creative impulses is no less central to persuading a client, a community board, or a potential patron of the virtues of a design proposal. Louis Kahn famously said that the main responsibility of the architect was to take the client's program and change it. By that he did not mean betraying clients' wishes, but rather understanding what they wanted and giving it form in a way the clients would not be able to imagine themselves.

However inspired an architectural scheme may seem to its author, it is likely to remain an abstraction unless the designer can express its reason for being in terms accessible to the people who must support it. Few of these people are likely to have architectural training. To those who simply wish to encourage good design, enrich their own appreciation of it, or teach its value and preservation to others, writing—like drawing—concentrates the mind on the search for the elements that distinguish mere building from what deserves to be called architecture. In short, writing—and writing well—on architecture is a skill that not only has promoted the understanding and creation of good design through history, but is also critical to its perpetuation in the future.

This book examines the role that writing plays in architecture, using examples from six genres: persuasion, criticism, scholarship, literature, presentation, and professional communication. The sources include some authors who are not usually considered to be authorities on the subject. Indeed, the selection is highly personal and limited largely to Western examples. Nevertheless, all of the texts are intended to contribute to an appreciation of the special place architecture occupies in culture: necessarily practical, yet potentially expressive of a society's highest ideals. The accompanying commentary and analysis is meant to help identify the strengths of the writing and to help readers strive for comparable results in their own writing and designing.

The theme linking all of the excerpts is clarity of thinking and expression. While a poetic description of a design can be compelling, it too often founders on the rocks of execution. Theorizing about architecture can be intellectually stimulating, but it neither keeps out the rain nor stirs the soul. A clear-eyed and literate explanation of architecture's special value to its users should be the greatest goal of the writer on architecture. When that goal is achieved, the buildings that result will surely be better than they might have been. And we will surely be the richer for it.

STRUCTURE

Even though you may start writing with a firm sense of the overall structure, you may stall if you insist on starting at the beginning. The first lines of a piece are essential to drawing your readers in and persuading them to continue. For that reason, they are often the most difficult to write. To avoid the pain and frustration of composing a perfect beginning, pick an easier part of the piece and start there.

CHAPEL OF NOTRE DAME DU HAUT
RONCHAMP, FRANCE
LE CORBUSIER

ONE

STRUCTURE
Getting Your Thoughts in a Row

LIKE THE ARCHITECTURAL design process itself, writing about architecture requires students and practitioners to concentrate on essentials and organize them in a coherent fashion. But most writers on architecture—or any other subject—tend to start typing in hopes of finding out what they want to say. Worse, they may persuade themselves that if they wait long enough, or do enough research, inspiration will strike and carry them to a successful conclusion by sheer momentum. Not a chance!

Every experienced writer learns at some point that disciplined application is the key to success. The Germans have a wonderfully expressive term to encourage students to apply themselves. It is *Sitzfleisch*, which can be roughly translated as "keeping one's butt in the chair."

The challenge for the butt's owner is to overcome

the anxiety that inevitably accompanies the beginning of any serious writing. Franklin Delano Roosevelt famously said during the Great Depression, "The only thing we have to fear is fear itself." The same might be said of writing. In a foreword to *The Elements of Style*—that slim classic of instruction in English usage—the veteran *New Yorker* writer and editor Roger Angell reminds us that "writing is hard, even for authors who do it all the time."[1]

Our educational system has made writing harder. We are all natural storytellers. When meeting a friend after an interesting day at work, we usually start with something like "You'll never believe what happened at the office!" Then we will fill in some background, move on to describing the events of the day, and wrap up with a conclusion about their impact. That represents the basic structure of any piece of nonfiction. However, when we turn to our own writing, our innate narrative skills are often frustrated by "rubrics," "prompts," departmental "guidelines," "accepted practice," and other restrictions that often specify too much ("five paragraphs," "two quotes per paragraph," "one-inch margins," "MLA style") without supporting the main mission of getting one's point across. If writing strikes fear into your brain and your fingers, you are in good company. But there are ways to overcome this fear and take some control of the process out of the hands of mechanical teachers, petty editors, and meddlesome bosses. An important first step is to realize that those teachers, editors, and bosses are not necessarily any smarter than you are. They have been on the job longer than you have, which means they are more familiar with the material, but there is no guarantee that their skills at architectural analysis or presentation are naturally any better than yours.

Most writers will admit that after they have resharpened all their pencils, rearranged all the furniture in their rooms, and reorganized all the books on their shelves in order to avoid touching the keyboard, they play a few psychological games with themselves to get the creative process moving. One of the simplest games is to take the number of words the project requires and divide it by the amount of time available to write it. If you are facing a ten-page academic paper, journal article, or presentation to a client, you may be looking at about 2,500 words, assuming 250 words to a double-spaced page. If you have two weeks in which to write the piece, and you take the weekends off, you have ten days available for writing. Dividing 2,500 words by ten days means that all you have to do is to write a page a day! (If you write more, you can reward yourself with a breather. If you write less, add an hour next time.)

But suppose, you say, what you write is murky and disorganized. What seemed brilliant at bedtime may seem lame in the morning. Not to worry. At least you have something to *fix*, and the process of fixing—or editing—will quickly take your mind off the fear that threatened to paralyze you at the outset. And no matter how much you have written, you get a regular (if small) reward. That reward is checking the number of words you have put down since you started the session, a calculation that computers can make at a stroke. If your final goal is 2,500 words, and you have written one page, you are one-tenth of the way home! And you can be secure in the knowledge that if you keep the pace, you will inevitably get to where you are going in the time allotted.

But you can *never* get there by standing still and waiting for the muse to appear.

There are two other sources of anxiety that tend to handicap writers on architecture at the very beginning. One has to do with the people you are writing for—your audience. Students often ask if they should have an academic or professional readership in mind. Every field has some level of specialty, and readers familiar with it expect to be addressed with respect for that knowledge. Lawyers, doctors, and other professionals all have their own "lingo," but that is merely a matter of terminology. What is "dispositive" for an attorney is simply "conclusive" for the rest of us. My recommendation is that you write for yourself—an intelligent, literate person with a strong interest in the material. You can always dress up the language as you edit, but no amount of dressing up will compensate for a lack of clear thinking and organization.

Another source of concern is style. After Ernest Hemingway began to write his lean stories of lonely heroes demonstrating grace under pressure, his use of short words and his lack of standard punctuation spawned generations of imitators. But the key to Hemingway's success was the clarity of his message about the relationship of his characters to their fate, not the prose through which he expressed it. In the end, style emerges naturally because each of us chooses words differently from everyone else based on our own experience with language. Without realizing it, you will develop a style that reflects your own personality; you should never try to be someone else.

Once these sources of fear are under control, the planning begins. The process should start with thinking through the issues and looking for an idea or argument. That should lead to an effective first step: creating a working title. This is not as easy as it might seem. If your assignment is to write about a new interpretation of Le Corbusier, your first reaction might be to title the paper "Le Corbusier Reconsidered." This may be factually accurate, but it is not particularly helpful, since finding an original approach to major architects is the goal of most scholars and critics. While something merely descriptive may be suitable for an encyclopedia entry, something more inviting usually is a better way to engage the reader.

An example is *Frank Lloyd Wright—the Lost Years, 1910–1922: A Study of Influence*, written by the architectural historian Anthony Alofsin. The focus is Wright's travels in Europe, which the architect was careful not to document lest he leave a record that critics might use to suggest he was not quite the original genius he claimed to be. The title not only describes the book's contents, but also provides an invitation to find out how Wright was influenced during those "lost years." Another good example is *Learning from Las Vegas* (1972). Written by Robert Venturi, Denise Scott Brown, and Steven Izenour, the book recorded their groundbreaking analysis of what they saw as the positive architectural lessons provided by the much-maligned Nevada "strip." The title tells readers what they can expect to get (information), but also that it is coming from a source from which no one expected to learn anything about high design. Don't worry about making a commitment by inventing a title before you begin writing. It is merely a device to focus your thinking, and it will almost always change as your research and analysis proceed.

Even though you are writing nonfiction, you can call on your creative imagination to help you get started. Indeed, having made up a title, you can actually accomplish a great deal by mocking up the rest of your piece in advance. This may sound heretical—or even dishonest—to some students, but just remember that the final product will be altered and verified by facts. Just be sure to identify your sources. The ease with which computers now allow writers to cut and paste documents has exposed even Pulitzer Prize–winners to charges of plagiarism, though the cause was usually inattention rather than deliberate theft of intellectual property.

A surprisingly useful tool in this initial creative process is the old-fashioned three-by-five-inch index card. While these low-tech items have lost much of their appeal since the arrival of the computer—and several computer programs provide a similar approach—the cards retain tactile virtues that digitization cannot duplicate. To illustrate this, consider the proposed paper about Le Corbusier. A common first step in writing such a piece would be to develop a basic bibliography, something many academic courses require even before you do an outline. The problem is that hundreds of books and dissertations have been written on Le Corbusier, and no writer can expect to absorb all of them without panicking. Instead, arm yourself with a deck of index cards and start putting down on each of them in a few words all the things a reader (such as you) might want to know about the subject. Those could include such fundamental information as the architect's birth and death dates, the design philosophies that influenced him, the aesthetic climate in which he matured, his critics, his admirers, his role in the design for the United Nations headquarters in New York City, and his expressive use of concrete.

Regardless of what you write about Le Corbusier, you will need to address most of these topics, as well as many others. However, you probably will not want to do that in the same random sequence in which the topics occurred to you. By putting them on cards and then spreading them out on a desk—or the floor—you will be able to shift them around according to which ones seem related to each other. For instance, the card for critics might go best with the one about Le Corbusier's work in India. Or it might go better with the aesthetic reception of his designs. His role in the UN project would mean nothing if you had not prepared the reader with some discussion of Le Corbusier's history in urban planning, especially the 1925 "Voisin Plan" for Paris, which would have eliminated much of the Marais district.

Moving the cards around based on these affinities will inevitably create a sequence for your essay. It would make no sense to include Le Corbusier's birth date at the end of the paper, and you would not be able to discuss his "Voisin Plan" without describing his contacts with industrialists. These are mere mechanical adjustments to make sure your cart is not in front of your horse. A more important outcome of this card game is that it tends to provoke thinking about the direction of the paper as a whole. For instance, if you find yourself drawn to the UN/urban-planning aspect of Le Corbusier's career, you may want to do enough research on the topic to find out what is, and is not, in the literature. If you are interested in the architect's activities during the Second World War, you might want to look into the way other artists (Pablo Picasso, Edith Piaf, Maurice Chevalier) dealt with the collaborationist government in power at the time. Without your noticing it, a theme is likely to emerge, and that in turn is likely to provoke a change in the working title. The original "Le Corbusier Reconsidered" might become "Le Corbusier and the Morality of Art under the Nazis," or "Le Corbusier's Urbanism and the American City."

A useful result of this process is that you will begin to sense how much research you will need to do on a particular aspect of the paper. This not only means that you will not have to read everything on your subject before you start writing, which is impossible; it also means you can avoid a dangerous trap. Since few writers actually look forward to the moment when they set the first words down on the page or the screen, many use research as a way to procrastinate. Generations of writers have persuaded themselves that if they read just one more book or article, they will be ready to write. But when the deadline is suddenly upon them, they realize that they have actually been putting off the main event. The hazard is that, while doing research is indeed part of the writing process (unlike watching television or reading mystery novels), doing too much of it is a waste of time, no matter how defensible it might seem.

At this point, you are ready to transfer the information from the cards to the computer screen. Writers who have never had to work with typewriters and carbon paper have no idea what a blessing the computer—briefly known as a word processor—has become. In times past, even a few changes to the text meant retyping much or all of a paper. Major changes, such as transposing paragraphs or otherwise altering the sequence of the writing, meant physically cutting the manuscript into pieces with scissors, reshuffling them, and then taping the fragments together before the retyping could even begin. Now, of course, these maneuvers can be done with a few taps of the computer keys. One disadvantage of the process is that we no longer have paper records to show how a piece of writing developed. So we have lost the opportunity to go back through drafts of a writer's work to see how it was polished and improved. But that is a problem more for scholars than for writers, who will never again have to deal with the physical burdens of editing on paper.

Writers who experienced the pain of revision through successive drafts had one advantage, though: they tended to think more before they wrote. That is different from writing and hoping that thinking will catch up. Seasoned teachers have told me that the quality of the writing they see has gone down at about the same rate as computer use has increased. This is because too many writers have come to believe that the computer can do it all—not just check spelling and grammar; adjust fonts, margins, and spacing; but actually think. Many of my own students have confessed that their process of writing a paper involved putting it off as long as possible, and then, when the deadline loomed, typing until the required length was achieved, correcting errors flagged by the computer, and turning in the result. Since the computer makes a paper *look* perfect (as it does some design proposals), the writer can be seduced into thinking that it *is* perfect. Not so! No amount of fiddling with fonts will compensate for advance planning and clarity of expression, just as in the design of a good building.

The key to success at this point is structure: how the piece is put together. If you have used the index cards (or a comparable computer program) to identify a logical sequence for your information, you are already in a strong position.

Many years of writing in various media on a multitude of topics have persuaded me that virtually all good nonfiction has certain basic components. A good prose essay will begin with something that brings readers in and encourages them to read further. There are many terms for this component, such as "hook" or "lead," but I prefer "invitation," because that describes to me the real mission of the writing at the outset. Most often, the invitation involves some measure of tension that must be resolved by the rest of the piece. An article on the nineteenth-century architect Frank Furness might begin this way: "At the height of his career, Frank Furness was the most celebrated and sought-after architect in Philadelphia. Less than a century later, he was the object of almost universal critical scorn, and most of his buildings had been demolished." The reader is obliged to wonder how Furness fell from his pedestal and can expect to learn the answer by reading the rest of the essay. Another effective way to begin is to suggest that the readers will learn something different about a subject on which they already may feel well informed. The writer might start this way: "Most critics and historians have dismissed John Portman, architect of such bombastic buildings as the Peachtree Center in Atlanta and the Marriott Marquis Hotel in New York City, as a careerist without talent. A close look at his positive impact on urban uplift suggests a different conclusion." Occasionally, a straightforward declaration will serve the purpose of engaging the reader, especially if it is provocative. An example: "Gwathmey Siegel's addition to Frank Lloyd Wright's Guggenheim Museum in New York City is one of the most blatant violations of a great work of architecture ever recorded."

Once invited, the reader will want a good reason to continue. This is the moment to preview your purpose or position. You don't want to give the whole story away—if you do, the reader may not read the entire essay—but you need to suggest the direction you plan to take with enough force to encourage the reader to keep reading. Many journalists refer to this section as the "billboard," invoking the image of a movie marquee with the names of the stars and some seductive quotes about the plot. Another way of looking at this component is to think of it as establishing the importance of your piece. Readers are entitled to ask why they should spend time on your writing. This is the place to declare, "Because you will get something you didn't know and can use." To continue with the Guggenheim example, the concluding sentence of the "importance" paragraph might read: "While most people would argue that even great works of architecture (such as St. Peter's by Michelangelo) may be enhanced by equally great additions (such as the colonnade by Bernini), there are some buildings that should be immune to alteration."

Once you have impressed your readers with the importance of what you are writing, you will need to provide some background so that they have the information to appreciate what you will be telling them. To return to the Le Corbusier example, if you have decided to examine the way his experience in New York City affected his ideas about urban planning, you will need to not only describe the architect's early plans for Paris, but also perhaps contrast them with the laissez-faire views of American real estate developers. If you were writing about Frank Lloyd Wright's "lost years" in Europe and their impact on his later designs, you would need to fill the reader in on the stylistic trends of the avant-garde in Vienna at the time when Wright was there. This section of your piece could be thought of as the background, or history, that the reader needs in order to follow your analysis or argument.

Your readers are thus now well equipped and ready to appreciate what you are adding to what may have been written about the subject before. To do that, you will need to cite examples that support your argument. But you need to be careful about the way you cite them. Merely listing information at random is a sure way to confuse the reader. To avoid that, you need an organizing principle. One reliable approach to organizing documentation is to move chronologically. Although a biography of the great architect Daniel Burnham might open with a discussion of his role as master planner for the 1893 World's Columbian Exposition in Chicago, the body of the text would have to proceed from his youth to his death. Another effective procedure is to go from first to last, low to high, or good to better to best. If you are discussing the quality of a particular architect's work, it would make no sense to begin with the later buildings and then analyze the earlier ones. If you are analyzing the critical reception of Edwin Lutyens's 1913 achievements in New Delhi, you would not want to start with postcolonial attacks on British imperialism; you would want first to lay out the goals of the architect at the time the project was conceived.

In discussing the Seagram Building, your topic might be the debate over whether in designing the building Ludwig Mies van der Rohe violated the orthodox Modernist prohibition against applied ornament. If so, you will need to establish how ornament was viewed by Mies's contemporaries. Although the radical Austrian theorist and architect Adolf Loos created a sensation with his 1908 essay "Ornament and Crime," he never actually said that ornament *was* crime. He just objected to the recycling of the kind of ornament that had been common in the past, whether they were Papuan tattoos or sculptures of naked ladies and winged putti draped around doorways. Well aware that even modern architecture had a responsibility to provide some visual interest, even if it had to adhere to principles of structural honesty, Loos exploited the decorative potential in the rich patterns of the marble he used in many of his residential buildings. The stone veneer in the dining room of the Strasser House in Vienna (1918) is as visually complex as any abstract painting. Nevertheless, when Henry-Russell Hitchcock and Philip Johnson mounted their groundbreaking exhibition *The International Style: Architecture since 1922* at New York's Museum of Modern Art in 1932, they made their skepticism about ornament abundantly clear. The exhibition catalog included a chapter subtitled "The Avoidance of Applied Decoration." In it the authors declared, "The finest buildings built since 1800 were those least ornamented." Of course, Johnson went on to assist Mies in the design of the Seagram Building, which drew fire from some purists for the architects' use of custom-made, nonstructural I-beams attached to the façade to create a visually interesting texture. Who was right, the architects or the purists? In either case, the reader should have been prepared to follow your own argument.

Nowadays, we take the need to preserve distinguished older buildings for granted. Thoughtful people would be horrified by the idea of tearing down the White House because it does not fulfill all the functional needs of a modern government center. But in the early 1960s, the owners of New York's Pennsylvania Station, the magisterial mock-Roman monument to rail transportation, concluded that the 1910 masterpiece by McKim, Mead & White was no longer financially viable. The railroad's president, in a letter to the *New York Times*, asked rhetorically, "Does it make any sense to preserve a building merely as a 'monument' when it no longer serves the needs for which it was erected?" The destruction of the station caused such an outrage among architects and historians that New York City passed the nation's first landmarks preservation law. But the owners of the station were neither stupid nor evil; they were doing what they thought was in the best interests of their shareholders. Few would now defend the decision to demolish Penn Station, but no responsible study of the loss of the building could ignore some documentation of the owners' position at the time. Whether the topic is ornament on the Seagram Building, or the fate of Penn Station, one could take a number of positions, but in both cases the writer must serve the reader by providing the context for the debate.

Inseparable from context is fairness. No matter how passionate you are about your subject or your position, you must keep in mind that others may not feel the same way. And if you leave out or dismiss opposing views, your readers will have good cause to believe that you are cooking the books. To persuade them of your position, you must address any reasonable opposition.

Few architects have stirred more controversy in the period since Modernism than Frank Gehry. The Canadian-born designer burst on the scene in 1978 by remodeling a 1920s house in Santa Monica, just west of Los Angeles. Gehry coyly described the original building as a "dumb little house with charm," but his reinvention of it was outrageously clever. Using unfinished plywood, chain-link fencing, and corrugated metal to create unconventional and unexpected forms, the architect at a stroke created a new architectural vocabulary. Many critics were appalled. It seemed to violate every standard of architectural design going back thousands of years. While it may have served the Gehry family's needs, it seemed to lack any sort of architectural substance, and its visual appeal seemed to be entirely in the eye of the creator. One of Gehry's neighbors actually tried to sue him over the look of the place.

But just disliking (or liking) a work of architecture is not sufficient. A responsible observer needs to probe the motivation behind the design. And Gehry had a powerful one. While he described his building as "cheapskate architecture," he argued that it was appropriate for its time and place. "I tried to see L.A. for what it was," he said. "If you look out the window, you could see everything as a mess—or you could begin to compose things, find relationships between shapes."[2] Seen from this perspective, his apparently chaotic structure could be considered an appropriate expression of a region that was prone to wildfires, earthquakes, and mudslides and where "building for the ages" seemed unrealistic. You might not agree with the architect's philosophy of architecture, but it would be unfair to condemn it for failing to conform to classical principles of design. Even readers who agreed with you would be justified in doubting the rigor of your analysis if you failed to explain that Gehry had deliberately defied those principles to make an architectural statement. In any writing on architecture, the author's credibility is the key to being taken seriously. Mockery, sarcasm, and invective can be powerful rhetorical devices, but if they are not supported by an even-handed analysis of the issues, they amount to nothing more than loud noise. While your readers may be entertained, they will not be convinced.

Let's assume that you have persuaded your reader of your position, which is the heart of your mission. A few structural elements remain. Much as we would like to think that readers read every word we have written, many tend to skim. That is one reason most accomplished writers devote a brief section toward the end of their pieces to a summary of their arguments. It is almost as if the authors were saying, "In case you were not paying attention for the past ten pages, this is what you need to remember." (Skillful researchers also know that they can cut their reading time substantially by going first to this portion of a piece, rather than starting at the beginning and proceeding word by word.)

Another common element in well-structured writing on architecture is a section that tells where what you have written is likely to lead. Just as good writers need to tell their readers at the outset why they should read a piece, those same writers most often give their arguments some forward motion toward the end. Mere description of the controversy that Gehry initiated with his "dumb" house would have limited applicability. However, if a critic were to end by suggesting that Gehry and his followers had fundamentally challenged the assumptions of centuries of received architectural wisdom, the writer could make a strong ending by speculating on the impact this challenge would likely have on the future. Will it produce more such sculptural experimentation, or a backlash of traditionalism? Just be sure to avoid the cliché employed by the many unskilled writers who end by abandoning all responsibility for what they have said by concluding that the resolution of the issue "remains to be seen."

Important as each of the structural components of a well-written essay may be, they can put off even the sympathetic reader if they are not assembled in a graceful way. Paragraphs that simply follow one another as if they were parts of an amplified outline can seem choppy and abrupt. Knitting them gracefully together is an important part of writing something that is not only informative but also a pleasure to read. If they can be reorganized at random, they are not in the right place.

There are numerous ways to ease the transition from one paragraph to another, but the most effective usually make a reference to what has gone immediately before, while previewing the material that is to follow. For example, someone writing on Daniel Burnham's career would have to not only acknowledge his impact as a planner and organizer but would also need to assess his architectural aesthetics. Thus a paragraph that follows a section on the Columbian Exposition might begin this way: "Extraordinary as Burnham's achievements as the mastermind of the fair may have been, questions linger about his artistic skills." If you are evaluating the impact of the demolition of Penn Station on the preservation movement, you might begin a paragraph by writing: "The loss of McKim, Mead & White's masterpiece was perhaps the darkest moment in the history of America's reverence for profit over art, but it was not the last."

Even though you may start writing with a firm sense of the overall structure, you may stall if you insist on starting at the beginning. The first lines of a piece are essential to drawing your readers in and persuading them to continue. For that reason, they are often the most difficult to write. To avoid the pain and frustration of composing a perfect beginning, pick an easier part of the piece and start there. An analysis of Burnham's career would have to include some reference to his professional training. Writing about that requires no special insight, but by recording simple facts, you will find that your fingers and your brain begin to loosen up. I like to think of Michelangelo's statue of David as a model for this approach. Genius that he was, the sculptor probably did not start at the top of his block of marble, making each curl of the hero's hair perfect before starting on the slingshot. By leaving the introduction for later and tapping away at the history, the development, the summary, and the future sections of your piece in no particular order, you will find that the work is beginning to take shape almost on its own, and a thesis is beginning to assert itself—like David emerging from the stone!

The only hazard of this "sculptural" approach is that you may be tempted to expand one section at the expense of the others. So keep an eye on the word count and remember that if one element gets larger, another must get smaller. Every now and then, check to make sure that your research is not threatening to alter your emerging thesis. If it is, then you can still change course, something you could not have done easily if you had begun typing before you began thinking.

Should you get stuck and wonder where your argument is leading, there is a time-honored writer's device available: close your door and read what you have written out loud from the beginning. Most often, the momentum of your prose will point you in the right direction. If you feel that you have read and reread your prose so often that you can no longer be objective about it, you can take an extreme measure. One established writer has been known to pin a typescript to a wall, walk to the opposite end of the room, and view the writing through binoculars for a new perspective.

So much for planning and structure in the abstract. In the chapters that follow, we will apply these structural principles to examples of writing on architecture by some of its best practitioners to see how their work may help yours.

STANDARDS

Absolute judgments of architectural quality are difficult if not impossible. Nevertheless, a rigorous application of thoughtful standards will help protect a writer from the lures of fashion and fads. Good architecture, regardless of time or style, has virtues that have been recognized across the centuries. Good writing about architecture is grounded in the author's ability to approach buildings with an open mind, sharp eyes, and sympathy for readers who may need help in appreciating the value of the built environment that surrounds them.

SEAGRAM BUILDING
NEW YORK, NEW YORK
LUDWIG MIES VAN DER ROHE

TWO

STANDARDS
How to Tell Good Buildings from Bad Ones

HOWEVER WELL ORGANIZED writers may be, their writing must be useful. Before one can write well about architecture, one must have something to say. Mere factual description is sufficient for program documents or encyclopedia entries, but to appreciate the importance of an existing building, or to inform decisions about a new design, the standards are higher. Indeed, they must include precise and accessible judgments about quality.

Many people are afraid to pass judgment on works of architecture, preferring to leave the choice to experts, by which they usually mean academics and professional critics. Yet while we can avoid literature, music, theater, painting, or sculpture, we are all obliged to experience architecture, whether in our houses, our workplaces, or our institutions. As a result, we are all entitled to our opinions about what makes a building good, bad, or indifferent. Developing a set of criteria is the first step in becoming a discriminating observer, designer, user—or, in this case, writer. And nobody should fear being wrong.

This became embarrassingly clear to me when I had just been hired as the architecture critic for *New York* magazine. At a party with some friends, I was asked what made the Seagram Building so good. Completed in 1958, this office tower on New York City's Park Avenue instantly became the poster building of high-rise corporate Modernism. It is included in most books on modern architecture, and it is widely considered one of the finest works by one of history's greatest architects. But why? I answered the question by mumbling something about how "everybody knows how good Seagram is" and how it is a monument of modern times, but I had to admit to myself that I had never actually examined my reasons for accepting the received wisdom.

Rattled by the realization that I might someday have to answer the same question to a less forgiving audience, I decided to do some on-site investigation. I bought a three-legged canvas stool like the ones artists use to sketch in museums, and on a sunny afternoon strode up from my office on Forty-First Street in Manhattan to Fifty-Second and Park. Nervously, I unfolded the stool on the plaza in front of Seagram and sat down, reporter's notebook at the ready. Braving the puzzled looks from many of the fast-moving New Yorkers streaming to and from their jobs, I forced myself to stay put for more than an hour. During that time I studied the pleasing relationship between the expanse of the plaza and the thirty-eight stories of the tower, which is set back one hundred feet from the street. I took in the contrast between the tower's palette of glass and bronze and the sturdy masonry of McKim, Mead & White's 1918 Renaissance Revival Racquet and Tennis Club across the avenue. At the same time, I came to appreciate how Mies, while using different materials, had understood the classical organization of the club and paid it homage in his own thoroughly modern vocabulary. I looked closely at the placement of Seagram's ornamental pools to north and south and wondered how my impression of the space would change if the pools were larger or smaller. I noticed that the edges of the vertical bronze

I-beams attached to the façade were curved slightly inward, softening the impact of the sunlight on them, and that the pinkish-gray of the window glass, while evidently dark enough to shade the interior, was not so dark as to block entertaining views from the outside of the office workers going about their business.

Feeling that I had absorbed enough of the exterior, I took my stool into the lobby and started the process over again. The formal symmetry of Seagram's exterior is echoed on the interior by four elevator banks. The twenty-four-foot-high ceilings create a luxurious expanse of space. I took careful note of the fine materials surrounding me: travertine walls, granite floors, spotless glass windows providing views of the people and cars passing by outside. I was aware that the lighting was inviting, but noticed that the light fixtures themselves were artfully recessed, creating an ambient glow on the walls of honey-colored stone. Without any scientific way to measure them, I sensed that the relationships among the elements were harmonious. It seemed that every detail of the space had been conceived to convey a message of elegance, tranquility, order, and power befitting an organization of great wealth—but one with high aesthetic standards. Folding up my stool, I realized that I had some answers for anyone who wanted to know why Seagram was so good.

From then on, I tried to conduct the same investigation of any building I was writing about, often returning at different times of the day and in different weather to see how it bore up under varying conditions. In my teaching, I ask my students to do the same, first taking in a building as an overall experience, and then boring in on its special qualities. The goal is to develop criteria by which the students can measure quality in a work of architecture. This is essential to being able to write intelligently about design, and the process is not as mysterious or as intimidating as it might seem.

The most familiar criteria for architectural quality have come down to us from Vitruvius (c. 80–c. 20 BC), the chronicler of Greco-Roman architecture who emphasized the importance of *firmitas*, *utilitas*, and *venustas*. These Latin concepts were first translated into English as "firmness," "commodity," and "delight." By "firmness," Vitruvius meant structural strength; by "commodity," he meant function or practicality; and by "delight" he meant aesthetic quality, or beauty. The first two of these are largely self-explanatory. The last of the three is elusive, since it is in the eye of the beholder and is therefore always open to debate. However, that does not mean that beauty is inexplicable. On the contrary, the aesthetic qualities of architecture are what distinguish it from mere construction, and being able to make a lucid case for what is in a beholder's eye is a major part of evaluating any design.

While the Vitruvian triad has endured for centuries as the basic criteria for judging architecture, other standards are also important. For example, does the building relate well to its site, including the buildings around it? The 1931 Villa Savoye, by Le Corbusier, is a landmark of modern architecture. Yet this austere white box raised on *pilotis*, or slim metal columns, is divorced from its natural setting and could have been deposited almost anywhere. Frank Lloyd Wright's Fallingwater, the house he built in 1935 for a wealthy department-store magnate in the Pennsylvania countryside, is perhaps the most famous private house in the world. Yet it is considered a masterpiece in part because of the way the architect integrated his building into the landscape, going so far as to bring the natural rock of the site up through the living-room floor. But his Guggenheim Museum, on New York's Fifth Avenue—also considered a masterpiece—is as alien a form in its context of stately apartment buildings as the Villa Savoye is in its country setting. Which is better? And why?

Beyond site, the writer on architecture must consider how the architect has dealt with scale, meaning the relationship between one unit of measure and another and the relationship of the building to the human figure. (The word *scale* is derived from the Latin for "steps" or "ladder.") A good way to test this is to study the parts of a building with which we are most familiar. The doorway to a conventional house is normally about seven feet high and two-and-one-half feet wide. This helps us measure the rest of the house. If the doorway is unusually high or wide, we instinctively sense that something is not right (unless, of course, the architect is deliberately distorting the relationship to make a visual point, as theater-set designers and Disney's Imagineers do). But if the building is a bank or a library, the reverse is true: an excessively small door would be both impractical and out of scale with the rest of the structure.

Closely related to scale is proportion, or the relation of a building's parts to one another. Does the building seem too tall for its width, making it look unstable? Or is it too wide for its height, making it look heavy and squat? The architectural writer Brent Brolin, in his book *The Designer's Eye*, conducted an exercise using computers to subtly alter the appearance of scores of buildings, both famous and obscure.[1] The goal was to demonstrate how subtle the differences may be between something that is considered excellent and something that is considered merely acceptable, or just bad. One of Brolin's most striking examples is the John Hancock office tower in Boston, designed by Henry Cobb of the firm I. M. Pei & Partners and finished in 1976. (Brolin gives neither names nor dates for his examples, reducing the influence of prejudice in the viewer.) Located next to H. H. Richardson's 1877 Trinity Church, a neo-Romanesque landmark, Cobb's glass-clad tower is cleft by a V-shaped notch that runs from bottom to top. This notch not only creates a dramatic shadow line but also divides the building visually into two narrow, asymmetrical shafts, thus reducing its mass and its impact on the adjacent church. The wisdom behind the notch is immediately apparent in Brolin's manipulated photograph of the building without it. As a solid block, the tower is overwhelming and boring.

The study of proportion goes back to ancient times and the classical concept of the *golden section* (a mathematical relationship between one segment of a line and another), but it has been pursued by every architectural generation since antiquity. The most notable example in the Modernist period was the Modulor scale, developed by Le Corbusier. He had been trained in the metric system and as a young man was fascinated by the latest products of industry, from grain silos to steamships and airplanes. A painter and something of a philosopher as well as an architect, Le Corbusier was frustrated by the metric system's unyielding rationality and was drawn to the Anglo-Saxon system of measurement based on the inch, foot, and yard because of its reflection of the human form. Invoking the golden section, Le Corbusier developed a scale of measurement that would (according to his rather flexible calculations) bring the Continental and the Anglo-Saxon systems together. This synthesis would not only produce pleasing architectural results but also forge a symbolic link between pure geometry and human proportions. In practice, the system had many flaws, but the attempt to simultaneously rationalize and humanize architecture reflected a recurrent urge across the ages to create architecture in harmony with the natural world.

The use of materials is another basic criterion by which to judge an architect's work. Perhaps no designer of the late modern period has paid closer attention to materials than I. M. Pei. The glass pyramid he designed as the centerpiece of the renovation of the Louvre museum in Paris is a consummate example. Completed in 1989, the severely abstract structure is the new main entrance, providing access to underground corridors leading to the galleries above. The architect's goal was to create a central feature that would have minimum visual impact on the imposing architecture of the original palace. His solution was to clad the pyramid in glass supported by a fretwork of steel struts. (A combination of Parisian air pollution and pigeon droppings compromised the hope for total transparency, but the pyramid is a striking addition to the museum and now competes with the Eiffel Tower as a symbol of the city on tourism brochures.) Pei was so determined to get precisely the quality of glass he wanted that when the centuries-old French glass fabricator Saint-Gobain said Pei's specifications were impossible to satisfy, the architect threatened to hire a German firm. National pride prevailed, and Saint-Gobain delivered the glass.

Pei's attention to the details of his buildings is considered a virtue by many, but obsessive by others. The Canadian-born California architect Frank Gehry takes an entirely different approach. His Frederick R. Weisman Museum at the University of Minnesota in Minneapolis, completed in 1993, is a striking sculptural composition clad in stainless steel panels. At a distance, the main façade, which overlooks the Mississippi River, is a powerful aesthetic statement meant to advertise the university's commitment to contemporary art and architecture. But on closer inspection, the metal panels in places seem to bulge and buckle at the joints, creating an impression of hasty, if not sloppy, construction. Gehry has always celebrated the theatrical and the transitory in his work, and perhaps the anti-establishmentarian treatment of his architectural details is a way of embracing the disorderly nature of artistic creation and contemporary life. Perhaps, on the other hand, it reflects a lack of architectural rigor. Pei's precision would be as irrelevant to Gehry as Gehry's focus on form would be to Pei. Who is right?

Whatever school of architecture may be favored at a particular moment, the best examples of it almost always demonstrate an internal consistency, or organizing principle. The architects who were trained in various forms of classical European tradition were expected to adhere to dictates of monumentality as expressed in the great works of the past. An example is the work of the firm Cram, Goodhue, and Ferguson, architects of the US Military Academy at West Point. Completed in 1913, the academy buildings reflect the firm's belief in the neo-Gothic as a style that perpetuated the spiritual as well as the aesthetic traditions of

Christian Europe. But they are also stripped to their essentials, emphasizing the underlying code of sacrifice embodied by the military.

The Modernists cast aside the overt historicizing of such architects as Cram, Goodhue, and Ferguson and developed an aesthetic that celebrated the machine, insisting that the sort of ornament favored in previous eras violated the honesty they felt was demanded by modern materials and building techniques. A powerful document of this is the campus designed in the 1940s for the Illinois Institute of Technology in Chicago by Mies van der Rohe. Using a modular system of rectilinear masses, Mies created a relentlessly orderly environment of virtually interchangeable architectural parts: without signs, there was no way to tell which of his units—all composed of steel members filled with brick panels and glass—performed which function. The chapel is almost indistinguishable from the research and classroom buildings.

In another turn of the aesthetic wheel, architects in recent decades have rebelled against the perceived rigidity of Modernist doctrine and turned to the sculptural possibilities provided by computer-aided design and fabrication. Underpinning many of these designs by such architects as Rem Koolhaas, Zaha Hadid, and Daniel Libeskind is a determination to engage the user through the deliberate use of spatial disorientation. While some of their buildings may seem chaotic and therefore lacking in any organizing principle, the careful creation of disharmony can, ironically, be used as an organizing principle of its own. At first glance, Gehry's Guggenheim Museum in Bilbao, Spain (1997), may appear to be a random sculptural form; on closer analysis, it provides a defining focus for what had been a disorganized urban backwater.

Good architecture is created according to organizing principles, principles that are intimately related to the message the designer wishes to send. Although the organizing principle of Albert Speer's designs for Adolf Hitler's Berlin may have been the sort of symmetry common to the Classical tradition, that principle was perverted by gigantic overscaling and simplification of forms to remind the users that the Nazi state was supreme and that the individual was both small and expendable. The message was one of power and intimidation. One could say something similar about American corporate architecture. Philip Johnson's AT&T (now Sony) Building, on New York City's Madison Avenue, is an example. While the apparently whimsical Postmodern split pediment at the top drew the greatest public attention when the building was finished in 1984, the oversized arcade at street level delivered the more powerful architectural message. Showing a troubling similarity to a design by a Nazi colleague of Speer's, Hans Malwitz, Johnson's arcade dwarfed pedestrians, reminding them that the communications giant that had commissioned the building was to be respected if not feared.

The US Supreme Court, the neo-Classical temple designed by Cass Gilbert and finished in 1935 (soon after Le Corbusier's Villa Savoye), might seem out of step with its time. Yet the message the nation wanted to send from Washington, DC, was that the central shrine of the American legal system was visually and unmistakably linked to its origins in Roman law. The same language has been used in the design of thousands of banks to reassure depositors that their money would be secure over time, just as the columns of Greece and Rome have endured through the centuries. More recently, Louis Kahn evoked memories of Roman vaulted forms in his Kimbell Art Museum, in Fort Worth, Texas (1972), perhaps subliminally reminding visitors of the expression *Ars longa, vita brevis*—art is long, life is short. However, what appear to be vaults are actually concrete beams in the shape of gull wings. The vaults have been sliced down the middle to admit light to the galleries. Is this an honest use of historical imagery? If not, does the sublime illumination of the interior not compensate for this bit of stage-set sleight of hand?

Generations of American students have spent their formative years oblivious to the fact that the collegiate Gothic buildings in which they studied at Notre Dame or Duke were designed to subtly enhance their education. A stroll through the courtyards of Yale or the University of Pennsylvania is meant to transport a student back to Oxford and Cambridge in medieval or Tudor times, when monks and scholars labored over their manuscripts in pursuit of knowledge. Of course, the Yale and Penn buildings were constructed between the 1890s and 1930s, but while their beams were steel rather than oak, their shapes and details were crafted to spur undergraduates to continue a venerable academic tradition going back centuries.

These criteria for measuring works of architecture are the most familiar, but they are by no means comprehensive. Each of us is likely to make some additions to the list. Among the standards my students have come up with are "intention," "sensuality," and "value over time." One student insisted that a good building must have "people at its center." He went on to argue, "Buildings develop over a long period of time and accrue a patina of all the people who have inhabited them . . . becoming part of our collective identity." Another felt that a building's design should "take an artistic stand." Others felt that a good building should address "the emotional needs of the occupant" and reflect "a thoughtful acknowledgment of constraints." Yet another argued that good architecture must "ennoble" its users and its surroundings. All of these are valid criteria by which to judge a building's quality, but the key to communicating how buildings fulfill these standards lies in close analysis and clear expression of the conclusions. As in the case of beauty, however, one observer's nobility may be another's pomposity, so the writer must be prepared to illustrate and document the ways in which a work of architecture conveys its virtues. Merely rattling on with such trendy architectural terms as "the materiality of an intervention," "temporalized signification," or "climax ecology" is not likely to persuade a reader, let alone a client.

Regardless of criteria, a responsible writer on architecture must take into account the intentions of the client and try to reinhabit the time in which the building was designed. Today's standards are necessarily different from those of yesterday. But one needs to be wary of the "Oedipus effect"—condemning one's parent before reaching maturity. In 1933, Rockefeller Center was damned by the leading architecture critic of the day, Lewis Mumford, who wrote that "the main building, from a distance, is a graceless hulk, and will never be anything better until it is hidden." Mumford went on to say, "Here one has monotony without strength and irregularity without any dynamic force."[2] Now, of course,

Rockefeller Center has been embraced by critics and the public alike. The entry on it in the *AIA Guide to New York City* reads: "An island of architectural excellence, this is the greatest urban complex of the twentieth century: an understated and urbane place that has become a classic lesson in the point and counterpoint of space, form, and circulation."[3] To take a more recent example, Edward Durell Stone's 1965 Gallery of Modern Art, also in New York City, was panned by the architecture critic of the *New York Times*, Ada Louise Huxtable, as "a die-cut Venetian palazzo on lollypops."[4] But many who might have agreed with Huxtable's aesthetic judgment nevertheless considered the gallery to be a representative building of its day, and such prominent architects as Robert A. M. Stern argued that it should be preserved as a landmark. (It was subsequently gutted and resurfaced.)

Changes in the way we judge architecture over time suggest that we must be patient about deciding which works to preserve and which to discard. Just as children tend to rebel against their parents and embrace their grandparents, people who make decisions about architectural preservation often undervalue the work of their own time, while rediscovering the virtues of buildings that have endured for a generation or more. Of course, if those buildings have been demolished as a result of changing tastes, there is no chance to reevaluate them free of contemporary passions. Merely because many orthodox Modernist buildings of the 1950s were considered cold and out of date by the Postmodern architects of the 1970s was hardly reason enough to tear down so many that, after a decent interval, might have been respected, or even beloved.

A building that survived rotations of the Oedipal fashion wheel is Paul Rudolph's 1963 Art and Architecture Building at Yale (since renamed Paul Rudolph Hall). When it opened, the building appeared on the covers of all the major American architectural magazines and drew praise from the most authoritative critics. Within a few years, however, its massive concrete bulk had become a symbol of all that was wrong with a nation consumed by racial upheaval and protests against the Vietnam War. Yale considered demolishing the building but was constrained by the cost and instead merely neglected its care. In 2009, having been recognized as a monument to an important period in American architectural history—and perhaps the best work its architect had produced—Rudolph's building was renovated and expanded. Its near-death experience was overshadowed by yet another outpouring of critical enthusiasm. Ada Louise Huxtable, who had condemned Stone's museum—and never changed her view of it—nevertheless recognized that architectural judgment is never fixed in time. Writing of Rudolph's Yale building in 1971 in the *New York Times*, she said, "Never have a building's fortune and reputation gone up and down so fast." She went on to observe: "How the human condition and consciousness change. How arbitrarily are reputations made, destroyed, and revived. How short is history today."[5]

The ups and downs Huxtable describes make absolute judgments of architectural quality difficult if not impossible. Nevertheless, a rigorous application of thoughtful standards will help protect a writer from the lures of fashion and fads. Good architecture, regardless of time or style, has virtues that have been recognized across the centuries. Good writing about architecture is grounded in the author's ability to approach buildings with an open mind, sharp eyes, and sympathy for readers who may need help in appreciating the value of the built environment that surrounds them.

PERSUASION

Like all the arts, architecture arouses passions and engages ideologies. But unlike the other arts, architecture affects every aspect of our lives. Persuading people of one's architectural convictions is a skill that requires an understanding not just of qualitative standards but also of the role of buildings as cultural messengers.

WAINWRIGHT BUILDING
ST. LOUIS, MISSOURI
DANKMAR ADLER AND LOUIS SULLIVAN

⊣ THREE ⊢
PERSUASION
Making a Point with Feeling

LIKE ALL THE ARTS, architecture arouses passions and engages ideologies. But unlike the other arts, architecture affects every aspect of our lives. Persuading people of one's architectural convictions is a skill that requires an understanding not just of qualitative standards but also of the role of buildings as cultural messengers. Perhaps more than any other form of writing about architecture, it also requires a *voice*. Persuasive writers must do more than present their positions; they must also sway their readers, just as politicians, preachers, and the best leaders do.

In years past, we have seen persuasive writing most often in the form of editorials and op-ed pieces for newspapers and magazines. But with the growth of technology, persuasion is increasingly the role of emails, blogs, and tweets. In all forms, the commitment to the message and the clarity of its expression have always remained the keys to success. And the most persuasive writers have almost always stayed close to the structure outlined in chapter 1.

Among the most durably persuasive texts in architectural history is the essay written by the pioneering Chicago architect Louis Sullivan in 1896, "The Tall Office Building Artistically Considered."[1] Sullivan was one of the most innovative architects of his day, but his commitment to design went well beyond the advances that he and his colleagues made when building with steel, glass, and elevators. Sullivan saw in architecture an artistic potential that approached the sublime, and his most famous essay could be read as a sermon on the skyscraper.

Wasting no time getting to his point, Sullivan invites the reader in by declaring in the first sentence: "The architects of this land and generation are now brought face to face with something new under the sun—namely, that evolution and integration of social conditions, that special grouping of them, that results in a demand for the erection of tall office buildings." An admirer of structure in writing as well as architecture, Sullivan moves immediately to "state the conditions in the plainest manner" and establishes the importance of his mission. "The problem," he says, is how to "impart to this sterile pile, this crude, harsh, brutal agglomeration, this stark, staring exclamation of eternal strife, the graciousness of those higher forms of sensibility and culture that rest on the lower and fiercer passions?'"

What reader can turn away from a call to greatness? The language is as compelling as any political stump speech and engages the reader in the writer's mission to find "a true solution." To help us along, Sullivan lays out in detail the components of the skyscraper, from the basement to the attic. But having dealt with them, he alerts the reader to a higher purpose. "We must now," he writes, "heed the imperative voice of emotion." The tall office building, he declares, must be "lofty." This loftiness "is to the artist-nature its thrilling aspect. It is the very open organ-tone in its appeal. It must in turn be the dominant chord in his expression of it, the true excitant of his imagination. It must be tall, every inch of it tall."

Having established his high ambition, Sullivan moves

on to develop his argument by undercutting those who might disagree with him, artfully dismissing them as "certain critics" and "other theorizers." This is a useful strategy for any persuasive writer, since potential converts will be reassured to know that the opposition is flawed or otherwise inadequate. Sullivan further stiffens his readers by summing up his intentions with his most resonant assertion: "that form ever follows function. This is the law."

That declaration has often been distorted by historians to suggest that Sullivan was concerned exclusively with technical performance, but his flowery prose, and the flowery ornament with which he decorated his buildings (much to the dismay of some Modernists who later claimed him as a forebear), argue for a man who included within the realm of function not just efficiency but also that elusive concept—beauty. He concludes his sermon with a canny invocation of an earlier sermon. By following his lead, Sullivan insists, architecture "will soon become a fine art in the true, the best sense of the word, an art that will live because it will be of the people, for the people, and by the people."

Sullivan's blatant borrowing from the final lines of Lincoln's Gettysburg Address may stretch the limits of decorum. But by invoking a historic call to national unity after a shattering civil war, the architect is emphasizing his dedication to a higher ideal for his art. Who among us after reading such an exhortation could ever again settle for a building that could be described as *short*?

Louis Sullivan's essay declaring that form must ever follow function became one of the most persuasive of texts in the modern architectural canon, but perhaps the most provocative was an essay written twelve years later by Adolf Loos, a Viennese architect in the forward ranks of the European avant-garde. Deeply frustrated by the decorative styles that dominated his city and much of the rest of Europe in his day, Loos lashed out with a screed entitled "Ornament and Crime."[2] (The title has often been misquoted as "Ornament *Is* Crime," an apparently slight but serious distortion of Loos's intention.)

Using the writer's familiar device of beginning with a then-and-now scenario, Loos starts by describing the culture of the primitive Papuan, who "tattoos his skin, his boat, his rudder, his oars, in short, everything he can get his hands on." Loos quickly moves on to "the man of our own times" and declares that "what is natural for a Papuan and a child is degenerate for modern man." No less zealous than Sullivan in his pursuit of a timeless law, Loos declares: "I have discovered the following truth and present it to the world: *cultural evolution is equivalent to the removal of ornament from articles in daily use.*" While those articles might range from shoes to furniture, Loos's primary target is architecture, and he sums up his thesis by stating, "We have conquered ornament, we have won through to lack of ornamentation."

Today we treasure much of the ornamentation that Loos despised; it is part of what makes Vienna, Paris, and Rome attractive places to visit. But a mere six years before the outbreak of the First World War, when European civilization was choking on its social complacency and militaristic ambitions, ornamentation stood (in Loos's mind, at least) for all that was rotten in his own culture. What better way to persuade his readers of his point of view than to associate the architectural style of the times with a barbaric society, one in which a member "kills his enemies and eats them"? Not content with this shocking comparison, Loos goes on to develop his aesthetic argument with practical and economic arguments, insisting that ornament is "wasted labour and hence wasted health . . . wasted material, and . . . wasted capital." While Sullivan invoked the people as the ultimate authority in his concluding reference to Lincoln's Gettysburg Address, Loos goes further. Wrapping up his diatribe, he appeals to a higher power in declaring that, "Lack of ornament is a sign of spiritual strength."

Both Sullivan and Loos are careful to refer in their essays to the views of those who disagree with them, and the authors are diligent in demeaning their opponents as ignorant or worse. Sullivan treats his naysayers with distant condescension. He cites "certain critics, and very thoughtful ones," who cling to the concept of the tall office building as derived from a classical column: base, shaft, and capital. He dismisses "other theorizers" for "assuming a mystical symbolism as a guide," and still others for "seeking their examples in the vegetable kingdom." Similarly, Loos concedes that ornament is not likely to disappear from Viennese society and that it is "joyfully welcomed by uncultivated people, to whom the true greatness of our time is a closed book, and after a short period is rejected." What civilized person would want to join their ranks?

Frank Lloyd Wright, the greatest of American-born architects, also advanced his strongly held beliefs by attacking the architectural establishment. In an article published in 1930 entitled "Architecture as a Profession Is All Wrong,"[3] Wright took up his characteristic theme of the creative individual battling the forces of mediocrity, represented most prominently by the American Institute of Architects (AIA). While writing was a decidedly secondary occupation for Wright, he adhered to many of the principles of exposition that we have been examining. He begins with a lament for the days when the AIA was "the soul of the profession" and architects "were individuals in their own right"—men like H. H. Richardson, Louis Sullivan, Charles McKim, and Stanford White. Following the then-and-now format, Wright declares, "Today it is 'The Firm'" that dominates design. And for "The Firm" he has no sympathy. Wright concludes his introductory section: "We know who runs the business but, unless unpopularly curious, we no longer know who makes the designs."

Neither as didactic as Sullivan nor as passionate as Loos, Wright nevertheless follows a similar development for his essay, filling in the details of how and why the architectural profession, in his view, has deteriorated: the "tendency to commercialize, centralize, or organize and standardize is expedient, or it wouldn't be here. It is profitable or it wouldn't continue." And he quickly leads the reader to his own prediction for the future: "Soon, individuality will be doubly desirable." When that comes to pass, Wright opines, "No system will be sufficiently adequate for modern conditions that does not give to the architect complete control of his design and assures control by him until final completion of the building."

Wright's larger target in his essay is the architectural profession as a whole, but at the end of his piece he returns to his bête noire, the AIA, reminding the reader that he had never joined the organization and recalling in particular an unscrupulous member who tried to block Wright's commission for the Imperial Hotel in

Tokyo in hopes of landing it for himself. Then, circling back to the introduction of the institute in his opening paragraphs, Wright slams it with a powerful finale, concluding that for him, A.I.A. came to signify "Arbitrary Institute of Appearances."

Writers who hope to persuade their readers need to acknowledge their opposition in order to appear credible, but as Sullivan, Loos, and Wright remind us, making the other side seem ignorant, primitive, or unethical is a powerful strategy. While these architect-writers were laying the foundations for a more modern architecture, Ralph Adams Cram, a tireless champion of tradition, was determined to dismantle them and return design to the realm of tradition. In 1936, forty years after Sullivan's essay on tall buildings, Cram published *My Life in Architecture*, one of his twenty-four books.[4] This stalwart of the Gothic tradition (he was the master planner for the Princeton campus and architect of its elegantly historicist University Chapel) had no use for the theories that were swirling about him from Chicago, Europe, and Harvard's Graduate School of Design, where the Bauhaus exile Walter Gropius by then presided over

America's version of Modernism. Cram's ideas remind us that not all architects in the early part of the twentieth century were content to follow the new directions being explored by their more progressive colleagues. Cram believed that architecture should be based on a reverence for architectural principles that had been tested over time. When he and his partner, Bertram Goodhue, designed the Cadet Chapel at the US Military Academy at West Point (1910), he was willing to reduce his version of the Gothic to its lean essentials, but he insisted on retaining a link between the building's martial congregation and its origins in what was known as "muscular Christianity." Indeed, the cross over the chapel's main entrance was rendered in a stone relief as the hilt of a sword.

Religious zeal was a theme Cram employed in a heartfelt assault on Modernism in his autobiography. In a chapter titled "Tradition Plus Modernism," Cram chronicles the development of the emerging trends in architecture in the mid-1930s, gradually grinding down their legitimacy through comparisons with the great works of the past. He leaves no doubt about his evangelical mission. Concluding his chapter, Cram writes: "It is unnecessary further to emphasize what I mean by the limitations set for the operation of the modernist idea in the field of art. It has its own place and it may and should go to it. Its boundaries are definite and fixed, and beyond them it cannot go, for the Angel of Decency, Propriety, and Reason stands there with a flaming sword." All writers should save something powerful for their final lines, but in the literature of architecture, Cram's warning about the apocalyptic dimensions of the coming architectural struggle has few equals.

However eloquent, Cram was a crusader for an architectural philosophy that had little chance of success. Someone who was able to slow, not halt, the advance of Modernism—at least in the realm of urban planning— was a diminutive New Yorker named Jane Jacobs. A journalist and activist with no formal architectural training, Jacobs lived in New York's Greenwich Village, a picturesque neighborhood of mostly brick townhouses and tenements that had long been populated by Italian immigrants. In the 1950s, Jacobs learned of the grandiose plan of Robert Moses, a city administrator with unprecedented power who oversaw much of New York's planning and construction, to put a super-highway through her neighborhood. Jacobs mounted a relentless campaign that succeeded in blocking the plan. Since then, the book she wrote summing up her views on urban development, *The Death and Life of Great American Cities*,[5] has become a classic that shows how a passionate individual with a gift for words can alter the received wisdom of the design elite.

In a chapter titled "Visual Order: Its Limitations and Possibilities," Jacobs addresses a recurrent theme in architecture: the degree to which design should be a factor in the growth of cities. The organization of her chapter is a textbook example of orderly explication. Like Sullivan, Jacobs begins with a provocative frontal assault: *"A city cannot be a work of art."* She goes on to explain that "although art and life are interwoven, they are not the same things," and sets out to "clear up this confusion." If we were to go back to the discussion of organization in chapter 1, we would realize that Jacobs has dispatched the "invitation" and the "importance" tasks in a mere two paragraphs. She then describes the ways in which architects and professional planners have lost sight of the virtues that make cities great: human interaction and visual variety. By trying to impose an artificial order on what she sees as the organic soul of the urban phenomenon, designers "make the mistake of attempting to substitute art for life." The result, she declares, is "taxidermy."

Stepping back in time, Jacobs devotes a section of her chapter to a brief recitation of failed attempts to regulate the growth of cities, from "nineteenth-century Utopians" and the "Garden City planning movement" to Le Corbusier's Radiant City and the City Beautiful movement, which she damns as "primarily architectural design cults." Moving on to the development of her thesis, Jacobs insists, "Instead of attempting to substitute art for life, city designers should return to a strategy ennobling both to art and to life." The heart of her argument is that "a city's very *structure* consists of a mixture of uses, and we get closer to its structural secret when we deal with the conditions of diversity." Before laying out specifics of how to do this, she reinforces her argument—just as Sullivan, Loos, and Wright had done—by impugning potential critics. "Literal visual control in cities," she declares, "is usually a bore to everybody but the designers in charge, and sometimes after it is done, it bores them too."

Jacobs's impassioned opposition to the conventional large-scale planning that was popular in many prominent universities and city governments in the 1950s and 1960s expressed the frustration of individuals with the bulldozing of what were then called slums. These communities often provided solid and inexpensive housing, and in many cases since then they have been rehabilitated as part of widespread gentrification. Indeed, there is some irony in the fact that the low-income neighborhoods Jacobs so vigorously defended in New York City have now become some of its highest-priced real estate, but one reason is that the preservation of a comprehensible historical matrix with aesthetic appeal makes a city a place where people of all income levels like to be.

Jacobs's campaign forced designers and planners ever since to take into account the advantages of urban "messiness" in ways no conventional textbooks on urban planning had considered. Moreover, it transformed the clichéd image of the "little old lady in tennis shoes" as the standard-bearer of architectural preservation to the status of an urban Joan of Arc.

In the wake of Jacobs's assault on the planning-based design of cities, the architectural establishment itself experienced a comparably devastating attack in print. It was delivered by Robert Venturi, a Princeton-trained architect who had worked briefly for Louis Kahn. In 1966, Venturi published a 143-page volume titled *Complexity and Contradiction in Architecture*.[6] Despite its small size, it had a monumental impact on the art and profession of architecture. Venturi's opening chapter was called "Non-straightforward Architecture: A Gentle Manifesto," but there was nothing gentle about it. Clearly fed up with the repetitive and predictable formulas on which modern architecture had come to rely in the years after the Second World War, Venturi took aim at its most cherished beliefs, among them that architectural history was of little relevance to modern design and that ornament— following Loos's supposed proscription—was anathema.

Like Sullivan and Jacobs, Venturi chose to avoid indirection and get directly to his point. In his first line he declares: "I like complexity and contradiction in architecture." Expanding on Jacobs's approach to urbanism, Venturi endorses an architecture "based on the richness and ambiguity of modern experience." Checking off what he sees as the multiple failings of "Orthodox Modern" architects (their fondness for designs that are "pure," "clean," "straightforward," and "designed"), Venturi wraps up the opening section of his book with a punchy line to emphasize the importance of his argument. "More is not less," he concludes, not needing to remind his readers that Mies van der Rohe's most characteristic aphorism about his own ascetic vision of Modernism was "Less is more."

While *Complexity and Contradiction* was published as a book, it is actually an extended essay, and it follows the structure with which we have now become familiar. Having invited his readers in with a radical declaration and asserted the importance of his position with a strong, if sarcastic, reference to a legendary predecessor (Mies), Venturi proceeds with an orderly set of definitions of the criteria—or background—that he feels his readers must have to appreciate his new approach. He starts with "Complexity and Contradiction," moves on to "Ambiguity," and then, using scores of illustrated examples from history, gradually develops his contention that Modernism abandoned vital architectural principles and that a new approach is essential. Employing the by-now-familiar device of using the same terminology in the conclusion as in the invitation, Venturi wraps up with the bracing assertion that "it is perhaps from the everyday landscape, vulgar and disdained, that we can draw the complex and contradictory order that is valid and vital for our architecture as an urbanistic whole."

While one can differ with Venturi's assault on Modernism and his prescription for a new architecture, it is hard to deny the persuasive force of his written presentation. The reason is that, like his earlier colleagues, he laid out his argument logically and accessibly. Starting with an arresting invitation, he asserts the importance of his argument, provides sufficient background to equip the reader to follow that argument, develops it with documentary examples, and concludes with a glance toward the future and a memorable closing statement.

One of the many polemicists to profit from Venturi's rejection of the recent past was Rem Koolhaas, yet another architect who launched a successful design practice with a powerful piece of writing. Born in Amsterdam, Koolhaas began his career as a writer for film, and that background may have contributed to his appreciation of the American scene. Venturi had become an advocate of American vernacular architecture, but Koolhaas embraced the country's messy energy, regardless of building type. The most eloquent expression of his feelings appears his 1978 book, *Delirious New York*.[7] Taking as his subject the island of Manhattan, Koolhaas is at his best describing the development of Rockefeller Center. With the freshness of an immigrant's eye, he lays out in delicious detail the reasons why, in his view, the complex of buildings succeeded despite the economic strains of the Depression, warring executives, and a design team made up of architects widely regarded by the aesthetic avant-garde as too commercially minded. Koolhaas's examination of New York is no less radical a document than those by Loos, Wright, Cram, Jacobs, and Venturi. Indeed, Koolhaas subtitled his book *A Manifesto for Manhattan*. But, like Venturi's, it was no gentle manifesto. (The cover image showed a bedroom occupied by two lovers in the form of the Empire State Building and the Chrysler Building in a state of post-coital exhaustion, with a deflated Goodyear blimp draped over the bedside like a used condom.)

The thrust of Koolhaas's argument was that virtually everything that Americans who had been educated in high design had been taught to disdain about New York City was actually admirable. Tossing aside Le Corbusier's Ville Radieuse and Robert Moses's grand planning, this foreign-born observer found Manhattan fascinating precisely because it was chaotic, largely unplanned, and intensely crowded. He opens his description of Rockefeller Center by calling it "a masterpiece without a genius." Having studied the ways in which persuasive writers begin their arguments, we should recognize the links to Sullivan's declaration that there is "something new under the sun," Loos's discovery of the "truth" in the conquest of ornament, and Venturi's declaration "I like complexity and contradiction." Like them, Koolhaas moves swiftly to establish the importance of his position: that the "essence and strength of Manhattan is that *all* its architecture is 'by committee,' and that committee is Manhattan's inhabitants themselves." Even Wright might wince at the embrace of group effort over individual talent!

Koolhaas then diligently records the history of how the unlikely midtown project came to be. "The seed of Rockefeller Center," he writes, "is a search, begun in 1926, for a new accommodation for the Metropolitan Opera." He then provides enough detail to impress the reader with the complexity of the task, pointing out that the participants were "alleged philistines." Of course, like Sullivan with "certain critics" and Loos with "uncivilized people," Koolhaas is setting us up for his argument that these "philistines"—led by the famously plain-spoken Raymond Hood, designer of the 1925 neo-Gothic Chicago Tribune Tower—created something that would have been beyond the reach of any single genius.

"In the end," Koolhaas writes, "each fragment of the structure has been exposed to unprecedented scrutiny and is chosen from a terrifying number of alternatives." Through the entire process, however, what Ralph Adams Cram might have called an Angel of Decency was hard at work, wielding his sword on the naysayers in the design establishment. "In the face of the Modernist *Blitzkrieg* of the thirties," Koolhaas writes, "Hood always defends the hedonistic Urbanism of Congestion against the Urbanism of Good Intentions." Wrapping up—although without any reference to Lincoln or the Scriptures—he concludes: "Rockefeller Center is the fulfillment of the promise of Manhattan." A few critics of the complex may still exist, but most people would agree that Koolhaas got it right.

While the writings of Sullivan, Loos, Wright, Cram, Jacobs, Venturi, and Koolhaas span nearly a century, they have in common a remarkably consistent structure. Although intended more to persuade than to inform, these examples of passionate polemics nonetheless are models of rational exposition. They all proceed from an inviting beginning, through a declaration of importance, to a review of the information that the reader needs to follow the argument. The authors follow this with a detailed presentation of their positions, usually undercutting their opponents along the way, before arriving at a ringing summary statement that points toward the future. While each of the writers has a distinctly different voice, all of them observe familiar demands of sequence and clarity to deliver their messages. Their delivery itself can be faulted in places for a lack of thoroughness or an excess of emotion, but that is often the nature of persuasion. It falls to the cooler practitioners of formal architectural criticism to move beyond polemics, and, by thoughtful analysis, form architectural judgments by argument rather than assertion.

CRITICISM

While the online era has provided almost unlimited access to information at unprecedented speed, it has also created a challenge: everyone is now a potential critic. Now that architecture—and criticizing it—has become an international activity, understanding the context in which it happens has become even more difficult.

PORTLAND BUILDING
PORTLAND, OREGON
MICHAEL GRAVES

-{ FOUR }-
CRITICISM
Aesthetics, Analysis, and Public Service

WHILE PASSION MAY HELP carry the day for persuaders with personal or theoretical agendas, analytical writing is a better tool to support architecture in the making. That is the role of critics. Not only do the public and potential clients need information about what is being built, but architects—at least open-minded ones—also can gain from responses to their work. One might think of the critic as representing the consumer in the same way that purchasers of products now routinely write online customer reviews. The hope is that architecture critics also have the knowledge, dedication, and writing skills to sort through their own views, integrate the consumers' concerns, and distill a useful judgment. As architectural criticism migrates steadily from print to the Web, circulating opinions from anyone with a computer and an Internet connection, the task of distillation becomes ever more challenging.

Indeed, while the online era has provided almost unlimited access to information at unprecedented speed, it has also created a challenge: everyone is now a potential critic, regardless of academic credentials or other qualifications. No longer must we rely on a few certified sources of wisdom at major newspapers, magazines, and journals. All of us have an equal opportunity to express our views to anyone who chooses to read our posts, blogs, tweets, or whatever platforms may come next. But not all of these sources are equally reliable. Too many bloggers indulge their egos, enthusiasms, and animosities without bothering to back them up. And since much of this can be done anonymously, there is often no effective way to challenge them. For that reason, it is all the more important that people who care about architecture be able to distinguish among opinions that are easily available and those that are valuable. In the past, we could rely on established authorities. Increasingly, we need to make our own judgments.

Whatever the medium in which criticism appears, the need for more of it (and at higher levels of quality) has provoked rising concern. Thomas Fisher, the dean of the College of Design at the University of Minnesota, noted that his experience writing for online publications had convinced him that even in the digital age, "the public wants to know what we have to say about the issues of the day." He added, however, that "architecture criticism is in danger of disappearing at the very moment when we need, more than ever, a searching and sustained critical conversation about the built world."[1] Fisher's alarm was echoed by Alexandra Lange, whose book *Writing about Architecture* opened with this declaration: "What we need are more critics—citizen critics—equipped with the desire and the vocabulary to remake the city."[2] Of course, architecture involves more than the city, but whatever its reach, architecture deserves intense scrutiny for the benefit of consumers and practitioners alike. Whether the message is delivered through a diminishing number of print outlets or through an expanding number of electronic ones, the key to making maximum impact remains—as it does for persuasive writing—clear expression. In the case of the best criticism, the reader requires thorough analysis and documentation as well.

Architectural criticism has been with us in one form or another for centuries, at least since Vitruvius. In this country, the earliest practitioners to attract regular readers were Montgomery Schuyler, an early advocate of the skyscraper, and Mariana Griswold Van Rensselaer, whose writings on Henry Hobson Richardson, among others, earned her in the 1880s the title of America's first female architecture critic. Professional architectural criticism emerged on the American scene with widespread influence only in the early part of the twentieth century. Among the most significant practitioners were Catherine Bauer, a proponent of high-quality public housing, and Lewis Mumford, who wrote for numerous publications and established himself as a leading public intellectual. Mumford was an elegant writer and was devoted to good design, but he took the larger environment as part of his definition of architecture. In 1921, for example, in an article for the *New Republic*,

Mumford wrote a prescient piece entitled "Machinery and the Modern Style" in which he declared that "the two main sources of the modern style at present are the subways and the cheap popular lunchrooms."[3] Mumford had the greatest impact at the *New Yorker*, where in 1931 he took over a column called "The Sky Line," covering such topics as the George Washington Bridge, parks, public housing, and the 1932 exhibition at the Museum of Modern Art that introduced America to European Modernism.

Mumford wrote his final "Sky Line" column in 1963, and in that year the *New York Times* took a dramatic step by creating its first position for an architecture critic, elevating the subject to a status comparable to music, art, theater, and literature. The first occupant was Ada Louise Huxtable, a former assistant curator of architecture and design at the Museum of Modern Art.

The appointment accelerated a growing national trend. Alan Temko had been writing architectural criticism for the *San Francisco Chronicle* since 1961; Wolf Von Eckardt joined the *Washington Post* two years later, followed by Robert Campbell at the *Boston Globe* in 1973,

Paul Gapp at the *Chicago Tribune* in 1974, and David Dillon at the *Dallas Morning News* in 1983. Gradually, architectural criticism had moved from New York City parlor conversation about the views of Van Rensselaer and Schuyler to the national forum.

But Huxtable, writing at the nation's most powerful newspaper, set the standard. She was widely considered objective and incorruptible, and her authority grew over the years because her judgments were well argued and well supported. She was also an excellent writer. A typical example is her review in 1976 of Houston's Pennzoil Place, a pair of prismatic glass office towers. With lean efficiency, Huxtable combines an intriguing invitation with a statement of importance in just three sentences: "New York architects Philip Johnson and John Burgee have completed one of the best big buildings in the country—not in New York, but in Houston. That is not surprising. Houston is the place where money, power, and patronage are coming together in a city of singular excitement and significance for the 1970s." Having analyzed the business goals of the developer (Gerald Hines), she argues, "This building proves once and for all that architectural excellence pays." She then concludes with a resonant summary and an optimistic prediction: "If Houston has found the formula for turning prosperity and growth into beauty and elegance, it is indeed the city of the future."[4]

Like most of Huxtable's criticism, this was more than an expression of her personal likes and dislikes; she was performing a public service by linking the aesthetics of Pennzoil to its role in the larger built environment—and to its commercial potential. Standards for making architectural judgments were discussed in chapter 2, but as Huxtable's example demonstrates, the application of those standards may vary with the circumstances and the context—in this case, "money, power, and prestige." It is to such critics as this that we must turn for guidance that goes beyond the Classical principles of firmness, commodity, and delight.

One of the hazards peculiar to architectural criticism is the critic's need for access. An art critic needs only to look at a painting or a sculpture to arrive at an opinion, and a book critic need only read the text. The same applies to music and theater. Few playgoers are much interested in how a play was put together, how much it cost, or what constraints the playwright faced in writing it. Restaurant reviewers are similarly unencumbered. No diner at an expensive restaurant confronted with a collapsed soufflé is likely to forgive the chef, regardless of the pains he or she took to create it.

Architecture is different. Every building that gets beyond the level of theory or abstraction must respond to certain real-world conditions. The responsible critic must not only investigate those conditions but also document the findings. It is not enough for a critic to demand that the readers accept judgments on trust alone. (Huxtable is not without sin here. In 2004, in an article about 2 Columbus Circle, a 1964 museum designed by Edward Durell Stone that was threatened with demolition, she declared with a seigneurial flourish about its origins, "I don't have to invent history; I was there!")[5]

The first condition requiring access is the program. There is no point in criticizing a building unless one has a thorough understanding of what the client and the architect want to accomplish. Attacking Rem Koolhaas's 2003 student center at the Illinois Institute of

Technology in Chicago because it does not look like the original campus designed by Mies van der Rohe in 1956 misses the point. After all, IIT had begun to suffer from a decline in applications and wanted to break away from what it saw as the dated rigidity of Mies's master plan and appeal to a new generation of students. Whether one likes the look of Koolhaas's solution or not, it responds to the client's wishes, and those would not be clear from the look of the building alone.

No less important is the budget. While Olympic Tower, a 1976 luxury apartment tower designed by Skidmore, Owings & Merrill on New York's Fifth Avenue, bears a superficial resemblance to Mies's Seagram Building, it is inferior in almost every way. Yet Mies had the financial resources of a family-owned whisky empire at his disposal, while SOM had to hope that its building would make money for its investors by selling space. Olympic Tower was a financial success; should it be condemned entirely because of its bland exterior and intrusion on its neighbors?

In recent years, as concern for the environment has increased, sustainability and "green design" have become major considerations for clients and architects alike. A critic who objects to the look of a building without knowing how its appearance was affected by efforts to conserve energy is not being fair.

No critic who looks at a finished building merely as a work of sculpture can make a useful judgment without considering these matters. To understand them fully, the critic must be able to talk to the people responsible for creating it. Such exchanges can be risky. If they go well, the critic may be tempted to sympathize with the client's and the architect's constraints, and that sympathy is likely to leach into a review. Critics who hope to follow an architect's future work must also be aware that a negative review of a building is likely to bar the door to interviews about the designer's next building. Not surprisingly, some critics inadvertently become unofficial advocates of the architects whose work they first favored, though they might not always support that work.

Paul Goldberger, who in 1982 succeeded Huxtable at the *New York Times*, gained a reputation for promoting the work of a small cadre of architects that included Philip Johnson, Robert Venturi, Robert A. M. Stern, and Michael Graves, while slighting others less well known. Many of his readers came to feel that Goldberger's reviews of the work by these architects were so cautiously even-handed that, while his conclusions often sounded authoritative, they said very little. An example is a 1982 review of the Portland Public Services Building, in Portland, Oregon, designed by Graves. The architect had become something of a rock star on the architectural circuit, but plans for the building caused a storm of controversy because of its blocky massing and aggressive Postmodern ornamentation. The *Times* critic introduces the architect this way: "Graves, if he is not an epoch-making figure, is the most truly original voice that American architecture has produced in some time." Goldberger goes on to describe the building as "a touch garish, especially with what looks like stripes of reflecting glass that run up the façade, but it is still respectful of certain architectural conventions that are the essential underpinnings of the classical ideal."[6] The assessment appears to be critical but is not so negative as to offend Graves. What may seem to be even-handed may in fact be a hedging of bets to guarantee continued access, and most architects understand the game. (Philip Johnson was said to have quipped that *Times* critics always had to say something negative in a review, just to maintain their credibility.)

The hazard of access applies not just to individual critics but also to journalistic organizations. Years ago, when the country had several major architecture journals—among them *Architectural Forum*, *Progressive Architecture*, and *Architectural Record* (the only survivor of the three)—each would compete with the others for special treatment from leading designers. If an architect could expect favorable coverage from one journal, the others would likely be excluded, and the competition among them for access in the next round would escalate, sometimes at the price of objective coverage.

Even if the impulse to praise a building is genuine and based on professional and aesthetic respect, unrelenting praise of one architect's work is likely to raise doubts in readers' minds about the critic's loyalties and undermine the credibility of the writing. Herbert Muschamp, the architecture critic for the *New York Times* from 1997 to 2004, had a special affection for the work of the Iraqi-born architect Zaha Hadid. In a 2003 critique of Hadid's Richard Rosenthal Center for Contemporary Art in Cincinnati, Muschamp declared in his first paragraph that "architectural and urban history were made" by this "amazing" design, and he went on to dub it "the most important American building to be completed since the end of the cold war." He characterized the building's appeal as "exquisitely primal" and insisted that the design embodied the architect's "historical awareness," concluding that Hadid "recasts the ancient story of cities in service to her time."[7]

The language is entertaining, and no one could accuse Muschamp of hedging his bets, but he provides very little support for his claims, and the reader is left wondering whether to trust an assessment that seems driven more by emotion (and Hadid's effective promotional efforts) than by analysis. When critics focus for any reason on a short list of architects, other worthy designers are left by the wayside, and the public and potential clients are left ignorant of all but the approved candidates for major commissions.

Even if critics strive to maintain a professional distance from their subjects, there is no guarantee that they are free from bias. Michael Sorkin, who made a name for himself in the 1980s writing for New York's historically left-leaning *Village Voice*, represented a populist philosophy that regularly brought him up against the high-design establishment. (Among Sorkin's most memorable articles was one about Philip Johnson's sympathies for the Nazis and other right-wing groups in the 1930s and 1940s.) In 2004, in an essay in *Architectural Record* that included an assault on Richard Meier's luxury apartment towers on Manhattan's Lower West Side, Sorkin concluded, "The ethics of architecture requires loving your neighbor, not dictating to her."[8] Nevertheless, other New Yorkers found Meier's buildings to be a welcome change from the normally nondescript architecture of apartment buildings, so a reader might ask whether Sorkin's commitment to community values clouded his aesthetic appreciation. The next question, of course, is: which is more important—aesthetics or community?

Politics can also play a part in the creation and reception of a critic's work. The career of the architect Léon

Krier was seriously threatened when he published, in 1985, a thoughtful reassessment of the work of Albert Speer, Adolf Hitler's favorite architect. (Speer narrowly escaped a death sentence at the Nuremberg trials because he insisted that he had an apolitical commitment to design.) In contrast, when Daniel Libeskind, a German-born Jewish architect practicing in America, designed a museum in Berlin dedicated to the memory of the city's victims of the Holocaust, few German critics felt free to speak ill of the project without risking condemnation as anti-Semites.

Time affects all critical judgments. No matter how hard one strives to write—or design—for the ages, the fact remains that excellence in architecture is neither a fixed condition, nor entirely relative. The proudly brutalist Boston City Hall, designed by Kallmann McKinnell & Knowles, was a critical triumph when it opened in 1968. Within a generation, however, it had become the most reviled building in the city, provoking calls for its demolition; a *Boston Globe* article in 2008 was headlined "Boston City Hall Tops Ugliest-Building List."[9] More recently, the quasi-Corbusian monolith has been enjoying a rebirth as a period piece of architectural optimism and has stimulated the formation of such groups as Friends of Boston City Hall, which are devoted to preserving it.

Not every reassessment produces a happy outcome. Catherine Bauer's embrace of Soviet and Nazi public-housing design looked embarrassing after the gulags and Auschwitz were discovered. And few critics are eager to admit their mistakes. Lewis Mumford, having condemned Rockefeller Center in 1933, changed his view in 1940, when the center had become a conspicuous public success, declaring it to be "the most exciting mass of buildings in the city,"[10] but never directly acknowledged his change of heart. Even so, we should be glad that even the most respected (and the vainest) critics can correct their mistakes.

To minimize the chances of a bad judgment, responsible critics should try to reinhabit the context in which the building was built. We still mourn the loss of New York's Pennsylvania Station, the 1910 McKim, Mead & White masterpiece that was demolished in 1963, virtually launching the preservation movement in this country. A less well-known example that shows how opinions of buildings can change is a dormitory that Eero Saarinen completed in 1958 for the University of Pennsylvania. An intimidating brick structure set back from the street behind a dry moat, it is widely disliked by today's students and their university. It does not even appear in many books on Saarinen's career. However, a search through the correspondence between the architect and Penn administrators at the time the dorm was being planned shows that it was exactly what the client wanted. The site for the building was at the edge of the Penn campus, near a then-unsavory neighborhood. Moreover, the residents were to be female undergraduates, whom the administration wanted to protect both from criminals and from the predominantly male undergraduate population. What better solution than to make the dorm look like an impregnable fortress?

A further oedipal footnote for the Penn campus is the university's library. It was built in 1890 to designs by Frank Furness, the most prominent and popular Philadelphia architect at the time. But it was later threatened with demolition because Modernist critics judged its gaudily ornamental style harshly. Saved by preservationists, it was renovated in 1990 by Robert Venturi, the godfather of Postmodernism, who recognized that what Furness had designed was a sincere expression of the aspirations of his time and that the mere passage of years did not invalidate it. The building is now one of Penn's most beloved landmarks.

The damage wrought by the intolerance of one generation for its predecessor was recognized by many critics in the 1970s. Among the most outspoken was Peter Blake, an architect and former editor of *Architectural Forum* who wrote *The Master Builders*, a tribute to Frank Lloyd Wright, Mies van der Rohe, and Le Corbusier. In his book *Form Follows Fiasco*, Blake issued a powerful mea culpa for the Modernist ideology to which he had once subscribed. After years of practice as a designer and a journalist, Blake concluded that "the Modern Movement—the creed in which we were raised and to which we pledged allegiance throughout our professional lives—has reached the end of the road."[11] Here is Blake's prescription to guard against critical error: "Since future functions are clearly unpredictable today, our buildings should be designed so flexibly that they

will be able to accommodate—and indeed, to welcome—all conceivable functions in years and generations to come."[12]

Such flexibility is a noble goal but is not likely to sur-
vive changing tastes and seductive ideologies. And no
one has indicted the persistent power of architectural
ideology better than Tom Wolfe, a journalist with a PhD
in literature from Yale. In *From Bauhaus to Our House*,
published in 1981, Wolfe endorsed the sort of attack
Blake had mounted on Modernism, but took it several
steps further. He accused the likes of Walter Gropius
and Ludwig Mies van der Rohe of belonging to a "compound," explaining that the "members of a compound
formed an artistic community, met regularly, agreed
on certain aesthetic and moral principles, and broad-
cast them to the world."[13] Wolfe's point was that the
architects who turned against Modernism had created
a new sort of compound, defining their own standards
and excluding the public at large. Wolfe had special
scorn for Robert Venturi, and for his book *Complexity and Contradiction in Architecture*. "At first glance,"
wrote Wolfe, "Venturi's words seemed rebellious. But

his designs never seemed anything other than timid." Wolfe supported his acid assessment with examples that showed how the so-called Postmodernists were creating an "architecture of infinite subtlety for the delectation and astonishment of other architects."[14] In other words, they were perpetuating the very system they claimed to be overthrowing.

Wolfe saved his most poisonous barb for the man who had become known in the press as "the dean of American architecture," Philip Johnson. Reminding his readers of Johnson's former role as "the most devoted Miesling of all" (for his part in designing the Seagram Building), Wolfe revealed the secret to Johnson's success: establishing ever-newer compounds ahead of the competition. Johnson's "trick," Wolfe declared, "was to *leapfrog* the new style and say: 'Yes, but look! I have established a more avant-garde position . . . way out here."[15]

Now that architecture—and criticizing it—has become an international activity, understanding the context in which it happens has become even more difficult. What newspaper, journal, or website has the resources to immerse a critic in the culture of another country long enough that he or she can reach a sensitive judgment? Architecture critics in the traditional print media are among the first to suffer from budget cuts. Most newspapers are even closing foreign bureaus and relying on "I-reporters" for what their own correspondents used to do. There is no architectural equivalent of the Associated Press, which can be relied on for objective reporting around the globe because its members pay to subscribe to its services.

At the same time, however, the reach of the critic is expanding—or returning to its early twentieth-century roots. Blair Kamin, who began writing for the *Chicago Tribune* in 1992, regularly goes beyond individual buildings to such topics as playgrounds for public schools, the renovation of urban subway stations, and the shrinkage of the suburban lawn. Inga Saffron, the *Philadelphia Inquirer*'s critic since 2000, has also widened the conventional horizon of the architecture critic by reviewing casinos and parking garages. Many *New York Times* readers were alarmed in 2011 when, after Nicolai Ouroussoff resigned as architecture critic, the paper turned to Michael Kimmelman, its art critic. The widespread assumption was that the decision was further evidence of the *Times*'s perception of architecture as an exclusively artistic undertaking. But Kimmelman has gone beyond his predecessors' fondness for aesthetic assessments of "starchitects" to tackle such topics as parking lots and the role of universities trying to expand against their neighbors' wishes. Lewis Mumford, that early analyst of subways and lunchroom design, might be proud.

Virtually all of today's print criticism is instantly available on the Web, and it is amplified by a proliferation of blogs such as *Archinect*, *Design Observer*, and *Log*, to name only three. But whatever the topic and whatever the medium, the same fundamental requirements of good criticism remain: fair analysis, documentation, and clear expression.

Those who want to move beyond the critics' "first draft of history" must turn to scholars for an analysis of the merits of architecture over the decades.

SCHOLARSHIP

Persuaders are allowed to rely heavily on opinion in their writing on architecture, and the best critics back up their opinions, but scholars face the added obligation of making dispassionate judgments intended to endure. An important role of the architectural scholar is to investigate areas that have been overlooked or misinterpreted.

ROCKEFELLER CENTER
NEW YORK, NEW YORK
RAYMOND HOOD AND OTHERS

-| FIVE |-
SCHOLARSHIP
Creating Meaning over Time

PERSUADERS ARE ALLOWED to rely heavily on opinion in their writing on architecture, and the best critics back up their opinions, but scholars face the added obligation of making dispassionate judgments intended to endure. The fundamental principles of structure and argumentation discussed in earlier chapters still apply. Scholars, however, must try to anticipate the hazards of the oedipal cycle and rise above the passions and fashions of the moment, locating architecture in a larger cultural context. While the roster of distinguished architectural scholars reaches back to at least 1800, the writers included here have had special impact on Americans' understanding of buildings and their makers. All are distinguished historians, but each represents a different approach to writing about the architecture of the past and interpreting it for the present and beyond.

We assume that scholars seek truth. That is why so many university logotypes include an image of an ancient oil lamp, the device that symbolizes the light of knowledge dispelling the darkness of ignorance. But one scholar's truth may be another's distortion. This is rarely the result of deliberate misrepresentation, but it may reflect the background and training of the person doing the research. So in writing—and reading—scholarship on architecture, one must be aware of historiography, or the cultural and generational context in which a historian works. No matter how hard scholarly writers strive for objectivity, they are inevitably influenced by who they are and where they have been—personally, professionally, and intellectually.

There are no better examples of the malleability of scholarly truth than Henry-Russell Hitchcock and Philip Johnson. Hitchcock was an architectural historian who taught for many years at Smith College and wrote the landmark 1958 volume *Architecture: Nineteenth and Twentieth Centuries.* Johnson, a wealthy and well-educated young man, at age twenty-six became the first curator of architecture and design at New York's

Museum of Modern Art. (He later earned a degree at Harvard's Graduate School of Design.) Introduced to each other by Alfred Barr, MoMA's first director, Hitchcock and Johnson traveled through Europe in 1930 and 1931, visiting the latest modern architecture. They returned determined to introduce their fellow Americans to developments abroad, and in 1932 they collaborated on an exhibition at MoMA designed to do that. Entitled *The International Style: Architecture since 1922*, it was accompanied by a book written by Hitchcock and Johnson with an abbreviated title, *The International Style.*

The book contained photographs and plans of the new work in Europe, as well as a few American examples, and laid out in its text what the authors saw as the main characteristics of the changing architectural times: "There is, first, a new conception of architecture as volume rather than as mass. Secondly, regularity rather than axial symmetry serves as the chief means of ordering design. These two principles, with a third proscribing arbitrary applied decoration, mark the productions of the international style."[1] Among the most prominently mentioned Europeans in the book were the

Dutch architect J. J. P. Oud, the Germans Walter Gropius and Ludwig Mies van der Rohe, and the Swiss-French Le Corbusier. The few Americans included Raymond Hood, praised for his McGraw-Hill Building in New York City, and George Howe for his Philadelphia Saving Fund Society tower.

The show and the book eventually contributed to a major shift in the direction of modern American architecture, but the presentation was hardly dispassionate by normal scholarly standards. One way to assess a scholar's point of view is to examine word choice. In the case of Hitchcock and Johnson, the words *control, pure, unified,* and *discipline* recur often as terms of praise. They are contrasted with such characteristics of the older architecture as *confusion, chaos, contradictory,* and *sterility,* to which the authors declare that a "single new style" provides a "solution." The effect is to suggest that Hitchcock and Johnson were less interested in chronicling what they had observed than in weighing it on a personal, moralistic scale. Their message was that the architecture of the past was bad, that the new was good, and that what was good about it was what these observers had agreed on. In a foreword to the revised edition, Johnson in 1995 conceded that the "moral certainty" he and Hitchcock had displayed in the 1932 book "makes it sound preachy and schoolmarmish. . . . We knew what was right and we were very evangelical about it."[2] Some of what the authors considered right in those days has either been demolished or is now in disrepute for its "sterility."

Apart from its righteousness, another criticism leveled at the Hitchcock-Johnson analysis is that it concentrated on stylistic criteria, editing out the social purposes to which many of the European architects were committed. Especially in the cases of low-income housing and factory design, many of the most progressive Europeans had been developing new ways to deal with the changes wrought by the First World War and the early years of the Great Depression, including a widespread weakening of the social order. Simple designs using inexpensive materials were the most practical and affordable. What attracted the eyes of Hitchcock and Johnson, however, were the forms without the social program. Suggesting a puritanical attitude, the authors praised Oud's work in particular for its "avoidance of picturesqueness, the severity of the composition, the perfect simplicity."[3] Yet these characteristics were largely by-products of attempts by Oud—who was for fifteen years the municipal architect of Rotterdam—to serve a social purpose, rather than aesthetic ends alone.

By providing a primer on the early works of the Modern movement, Hitchcock and Johnson performed a major service to American architecture. In the process, however, they admitted to their fraternity only those whose work conformed to their definition of the specific style they admired. They did not include Frank Lloyd Wright, even though the monograph of his work published in Berlin in 1910 had been a major inspiration for many European Modernists. Because Wright had no use for stylistic labels, and because his work did not fit their rigid framework, the authors dismissed him by saying, "One cannot deny that among the architects of the older generation Wright made more contributions than any other."[4] For some decades, in the absence of an equally clear account of this movement, this qualified as scholarship of a sort, but it was really advocacy and criticism.

Unlike Hitchcock and Johnson, Talbot Hamlin made no apologies for America's architectural legacy. Trained in English and classics, Hamlin earned an architecture degree from Columbia and went into practice before returning to his university, where he taught architectural history and became head of the Avery Architectural Library, still one of the country's richest resources for scholarly architectural material. He was also a cofounder of the Society of Architectural Historians. Hamlin's *Architecture through the Ages*, published in 1940, was, as the title suggests, a sweeping history of the subject, but it was more than a mere recitation of facts. In his chapter "The Classic Revival in the United States," Hamlin displayed in his account of the rise and fall of an architectural idea the sort of skill the best historians possess at being able to invest events with meaning. In his first paragraph, Hamlin wrote: "The inspiration of Rome and Greece belonged to the Americans of the time as much as it did to the Europeans, for were they not all children of the same basic heritage? And the ideals of Roman republican austerity, of Greek democratic enlightenment, were ideals most congenial to the

American spirit of the period. The New World should have a new architecture as grand as that of Rome, as delicate and lovely as the architecture of Greece."[5] With this eloquent opening, Hamlin invited the reader to discover how it was that the young United States employed Classical traditions.

Like most good writers, however, Hamlin does not give his whole story away at the beginning. After a review of the major buildings of the Greek Revival in America, Hamlin chronicles the decline of the movement. He does so by explaining how more than style was involved. Returning to his cultural analysis of the original appeal of Classical precedents to Americans, he explains how the changing nature of their society demanded a search for new forms. "The Greek Revival," Hamlin writes in his closing paragraph,

> died because other influences stronger than any mere
> architectural fashion were more and more becoming the
> governing qualities of American life. . . . The old feeling
> of the aristocracy of the learned, of the professional class,
> was giving way rapidly to a new feeling of the dominance
> of wealth. It had been the lawyer and the minister who

*had ruled; now it was the wealthy industrialist. In such
a society the old standards ceased to command; the
new plutocracy sought architectural expressions more
ostentatious, more blatant, than the careful harmonies
and the muted details of the older type. And they wanted
results in a hurry.*[6]

Hamlin's nostalgia for the passing of the old standards became even clearer in a later work, *Greek Revival
Architecture in America*, published in 1944. The dedication of the book reads, in part: "To all those architects
and planners who today are creating the forms that
embody the American dream." Here one can detect
a cause for concern about Hamlin's work similar to
the one represented by Hitchcock and Johnson. While
Hamlin strove objectively to survey the entire history
of architecture, he was clearly partial to the Classical,
whether in its original or revived form, and he had little
use for Modernism. In the chapter titled "The Architecture of Today" in *Architecture through the Ages*, there
is no mention of the MoMA International Style show,
even though it took place only a few miles from the
Columbia campus and fully eight years before his oth-

erwise comprehensive survey was published. This may not diminish Hamlin's stature as a scholar, but it is a reminder that personal and scholarly preferences may subtly tip the scale of even-handedness.

One important role of the architectural scholar is to investigate areas that have been overlooked or misinterpreted. Carl Condit, who taught at Northwestern University from 1947 to 1982, made a lasting contribution to the writing of American architectural history by emphasizing the part played by technology, especially in Chicago. Some scholars writing on the subject have been eager to compensate for the relative lack of attention paid to technical matters by suggesting that architecture is merely window-dressing for engineering. While championing engineering's importance, Condit charted a nuanced course that acknowledged the complementary—and sometimes conflicting—roles played by each. Like Hamlin on Classical principles, Condit also situated the issues in the cultural context of a growing United States.

Condit's major work was *The Chicago School of Architecture* (1964), which established him as the leading authority on the history of building technology in America. In his chapter "Adler and Sullivan," on the extraordinary partnership of Dankmar Adler and Louis Sullivan, Condit concentrated on a selection of their buildings but used them to illustrate a theme with relevance well beyond Chicago of the late nineteenth century. In his discussion of Adler and Sullivan's Wainwright Building in St. Louis, completed in 1891, he devotes a passage to Sullivan's use of recessed spandrels, ornament, and red brick on the façades: "This personal treatment of the elevations in a sculptural way reveals Sullivan's feeling for the tall building to be strictly subjective and somewhat at odds with what one might call the more neutral and empirical character of the main body of Chicago work. His approach might be characterized as the higher functionalism of psychological as well as utilitarian statement."[7] In two deft sentences, Condit both links Sullivan to his regional context and identifies his uniqueness as an artist.

Later in the same chapter, Condit again selects a single structure, the 1892 Schiller Building—later the Garrick Theater—to make a larger point. Discussing the unsuccessful attempts to save the technologically innovative building from demolition, Condit notes, "The practical exigencies involved in attempts to preserve a large building in a badly deteriorated condition and the legal issues arising from compensation to the owners brought the problem of the Garrick Theater to a perfect impasse."[8] He goes on to say: "The basic truth is that there is a fundamental contradiction in the United States between the aims of commercial enterprise and the values of aesthetic achievement."[9] With an efficiency that any engineer might admire, Condit has used the example of a single building to focus the reader's attention on one of the most vexing and durable issues in architecture: what to preserve and why. But where many writers might indulge in self-righteous attacks on the philistinism of the building's owners or the venality of politicians, Condit has dispassionately presented the issues so that a reader can come to a balanced conclusion. While Condit's scholarly reputation may rest primarily on his campaign to recognize the importance of technology in American architecture, it should also reflect his rare degree of intellectual fairness.

No other American architectural historian has achieved such public recognition as Vincent Scully. He taught at Yale from 1947 until his retirement in 1991. The author of numerous books, Scully in 1995 was invited to deliver the Jefferson Lecture, the federal government's highest recognition in the humanities, and in 2004 he was awarded the National Medal of Arts. The citation for the medal read: "For his remarkable contributions to the history of design and modern architecture, including his influential teaching as an architectural historian."

As a teacher, Scully electrified generations of students with his theatrical slide lectures, which ranged from prehistoric sculpture to the latest skyscrapers. They were often conducted in total darkness so that students would have to concentrate on his images and his words rather than on their notes. Scully had a sharp eye for emerging talent and was the first major scholar to identify the importance of Louis Kahn and, later, Robert Venturi.

Central to Scully's interpretation of architectural history was a conviction that recalled the "archetypes" of the psychologist Carl Jung, who believed that certain forms and principles have universal meaning across cultures. In his 1991 book *Architecture: The Natural and the Manmade*, Scully argues that the Ancients located their temples with special attention to their natural surroundings, which he describes in a style all his own: "On the Sacred Way from Athens, for example, the island of Salamis, dedicated to Aphrodite, a goddess of mountain and sea, lies directly ahead, deeply cleft and horned."[10] Writing about the gods to whom the temples were dedicated, Scully invokes Jungian themes when he says, "Any modern man who says he does not know them does not know his own mind, because, if he has tried to deal with the realities of things as they are, the appropriate Greek gods have been there with him in their power: Aphrodite in love, Apollo in clear reasoning, Dionysos in ecstatic possession, Zeus in justice, Athena in right action and divine effrontery, Ares, the big-kneed, in the loutish skills of war."[11]

Although Scully did much of his early scholarship on Greek architecture, he later expanded his geographical reach without abandoning his core convictions. In describing the Native American architecture of the

Southwest, Scully declared: "The architectural principle at work in these individual dwellings . . . is that of the imitation of natural forms by human beings who seek thereby to fit themselves safely into nature's order."[12] Ranging from the pyramids in Egypt and Central America to the skyscrapers of Lower Manhattan, and positing artistic and spiritual links among them all, Scully insisted: "So human beings reinforce the landscape's forms, focus them, wind them up to work as they damn well ought to do."[13]

Scant documentation exists to support Scully's assertions, and in *Architecture: The Natural and the Manmade* the author even dispenses with footnotes and bibliography, but his arguments carry such intuitive force that one hopes they are true. And however questionable from the point of view of conventional scholarly practice, Scully's boundless enthusiasm and emotional interpretation were irresistible to legions of his students, many of whom went on to make major contributions to American architecture, especially by writing about it. (Among Scully's alumni are the late Spiro Kostof of the University of California at Berkeley, author of *A History of Architecture: Settings and Rituals*; Neil Levine, in the art history department at Harvard and author of *The Architecture of Frank Lloyd Wright*; David McCullough, whose *The Great Bridge* is the definitive account of Brooklyn's best-known monument; Marvin Trachten-berg of New York University's Institute of Fine Arts; and two Pulitzer Prize–winning critics, Paul Goldberger, formerly of the *New York Times* and the *New Yorker*, and Blair Kamin of the Chicago *Tribune*.)

Like Scully, William Jordy received his PhD from Yale, and he taught there until 1955. Then he left for Brown, where he remained until his death in 1997. Jordy collab-orated with William Pierson of Williams College on the series of volumes with the main title *American Buildings and Their Architects*, creating a definitive body of schol-arship on the topic. Both were admirable writers, but a selection from Jordy is most relevant here for the way in which he wrote about the larger cultural significance of a building that Hitchcock and Johnson had considered from a more limited point of view in *The International Style*. While Jordy never attained the public acclaim that Scully did, his dogged pursuit of verifiable information and fair judgment created a body of writing that remains among the most respected in his field.

Jordy's final *American Buildings and Their Architects* volume was subtitled *The Impact of European Modernism in the Mid-Twentieth Century*. Primary among the examples Jordy selected to illustrate that impact is the Philadelphia Saving Fund Society (PSFS) tower in Philadelphia, designed by George Howe and his Swiss-born partner William Lescaze, and one of the few American buildings illustrated by Hitchcock and Johnson. But unlike his colleagues, Jordy does not use the building as evidence to demonstrate the rightness of an aesthetic argument. Instead he considers it analytically, situating it in the evolution of American architecture. And he does it by adhering to principles of writing with which we have now become familiar.

Jordy opens his consideration of the PSFS tower with a standard device, referring to his preceding chapter on New York's Rockefeller Center but pointing out a contrast: "Whereas Rockefeller Center exemplifies Beaux-Arts ideals becoming modern, Howe & Lescaze's contemporary skyscraper for the Philadelphia Saving

Fund Society (1929–1932) is fully committed to European modernism as this developed in the twenties."[14] This is a reliable then-and-now beginning, which Jordy rapidly follows with a statement of why readers should keep reading: "In the development of the bare-bones esthetic of modern skyscraper design, PSFS is the most important tall building erected between the Chicago School of the eighteen eighties and the metal-and-glass revival beginning around 1950."[15]

Jordy then goes into the demand of the building's client for an "ultra-Practical" structure that would enhance the bank's image as forward-looking but would also represent a "sound investment."[16] Having analyzed the ways in which the architects chose to give these aspirations physical form, Jordy compares the building to recent work by the European Modernists, but concludes with a powerful description of the special position of PSFS in the American architectural trajectory. "In fact," he writes,

> *the uniqueness of PSFS, both as a building and as*
> *an historical event, appears in its extraordinary*
> *ambiguity, as reconciliation, synthesis, and prophecy.*
> *It reconciles the rationalism of the academic tradition*

with that of the modern movement. It synthesizes both
brands of rationalism with a comprehensive view of the
International Style, the functional, expressionist, and
constructivist modes of which are especially evident
in a startlingly dichotomous union of container and
component. It prophesies developments of special
consequence in modern American architecture in its bold
revelation of the projecting structural columns and its
discreet compartmentalization of functions.[17]

Observing a writerly respect for structural symmetry, Jordy then returns to the language he used at the beginning of his chapter to drive home his original point about PSFS: "For these reasons and for its intrinsic quality, it stands as the most important American skyscraper between Sullivan's work of the nineties . . . and the Seagram Building at the end of the fifties, all rooted in rationalistic philosophies of architecture."[18] While Scully asserts his points through personal associations and passionate rhetoric, Jordy has diligently assembled the evidence for PSFS's importance with such care that most readers can come to no other conclusion than his—and may even think that they came to it on their own.

One of the hazards of scholarship is that it assumes a steady process of discovery. Often this involves reexamination of work by earlier scholars, and often those new perspectives advance our understanding by revealing oversights or new information. In some cases, however, the reexamination may reassemble facts in new frames to make the material appear fresh even when it remains largely unchanged.

In an ambitious reconsideration of American twentieth-century architectural history entitled simply *USA*, Gwendolyn Wright—the first woman to be granted tenure at Columbia's Graduate School of Architecture, Planning and Preservation—set out to correct what she saw as an imbalance in that history. Central to the scholarship Wright was revisiting was, in her view, an inappropriate emphasis on prominent architects and established standards of quality. In her introduction, Wright says: "I am suggesting an inclusive, dynamic and contested perspective, not a harmonious consensus."[19] She goes on to say: "Rather than simply describing stars I highlight the constellations that can be read in multiple ways and seen from different perspectives."[20]

In reviewing the history of American architecture, Wright concentrates her attention on groups that have often been overlooked or slighted, especially women and minorities. She notes that the same nineteenth-century technological advances that contributed to the buildings Carl Condit celebrated also aggravated social inequities. "New equipment," Wright explains, "helped generate a female clerical force whose members became interchangeable elements arrayed in rows in large central areas under the scrutiny of male managers."[21] She provides a new perspective on the domestic designs of America's most famous architect: "Following the tenets of Chicago progressives, especially women reformers, Wright integrated work and family life under one roof."[22] While identifying formerly overlooked aspects of American architecture's impact on women, Wright also turns a fresh eye on its racial dimension. She observes that in the 1930s the policies of the Federal Housing Administration reflected an "endorsement of racial segregation as part of sound 'neighborhood planning'—a position that lasted until 1968."[23]

While Wright's analysis of American architecture is

informative and in many ways refreshing, an examination of her word choice and illustrative examples reveals a partisanship much like that which Hitchcock and Johnson showed for European Modernism, Hamlin for the Classical Revival, and Scully for Jungian universalism. An early clue is Wright's declaration that "Americans have become increasingly distrustful of the modern state with its inflated bureaucracies, conspicuous corruption, wasteful profligacy and increased surveillance."[24] She has little patience for the many prominent architects who, she asserts, suffer from "narcissistic nonchalance" and "followed the money to Asia." Nonprofit organizations, however, tend to be "innovative," while "feminists reclaimed the domestic realm as a site to negotiate the everyday practices of modernity,"[25] and a few underrepresented architects produce "resourceful, exuberant design."[26]

Following an era in American architecture that might well be described as one of wretched excess, Wright's corrective scholarship is welcome. But by indulging in familiar characterizations of power and patronage—

whether represented by government, industry, or personal wealth—Wright seems unwilling to fully accept that much great architecture emerged with their help. While positive social goals are noble, they do not always generate high art. Wright's book serves architectural scholarship well by drawing attention to the excesses of modern society as expressed in its buildings and reminding us that traditional standards need to be continuously tested for their soundness. However, her conspicuous commitment to social justice should alert her readers to the impact it may have had on her judgment of architecture's aesthetic importance.

Wright—like Hitchcock, Johnson, Hamlin, Condit, Scully, and Jordy—is part of an ongoing scholarly tradition. Its goal is to distill durable meaning from architectural fact. No writer can entirely escape context or influence in pursuing that goal, but the good ones try. Their best work endures to the degree that it strives to avoid prejudice, even if some prejudices are unavoidable, or even desirable as a way of opening new perspectives on familiar scenes.

In another realm—that of literature—writers on architecture need observe no such constraints. They are free to enhance the facts with imagination and artistry, carrying our understanding of the built environment beyond information to enjoyment—even to inspiration.

LITERATURE

Architecture provides settings for much of the world's greatest literature. Factual and interpretive description of architecture aside, literature has the advantage of tapping into our imaginations and emotions. Creative writers can enrich our appreciation of the built world in ways that the mere recording and analysis of data cannot.

BRUNELLESCHI'S DOME
FLORENCE, ITALY
FILIPPO BRUNELLESCHI

SIX

LITERATURE
The Heart of the Matter

ARCHITECTURE PROVIDES SETTINGS for much of the world's great literature. In Homer's *Iliad*, Achilles and Hector clash on the plains before the "fair battlements" of "high-gated Troy." Victor Hugo's hunchbacked Quasimodo finds a home in the cathedral of Notre Dame. Like Troy, the brooding structure in Franz Kafka's psychological classic *The Castle* also has battlements, but these are "uncertain, irregular, brittle, as if drawn by the anxious or careless hand of a child."[1]

The types of writing analyzed in the preceding chapters relied on the factual and interpretive description of architecture, but literature has the advantage of tapping into our imaginations and emotions. A novelist, a travel writer, or even a writer of espionage thrillers can indulge in imagery and artistic license to evoke the spirit and feeling of a building or a place. Those who do it well can enrich our appreciation of the built world in ways that the mere recording and analysis of data cannot. The examples that follow reflect only a small sampling of authorial voices and points of view, but they are all reminders that writing about architecture can go well beyond the facts.

As America's most revered satirist, Mark Twain was a master of physical description as a vehicle for social commentary. In *The Adventures of Huckleberry Finn*, Huck, his rowboat sunk by a Mississippi steamer, stumbles ashore and comes upon "a big old-fashioned double log house." Huck knocks on the door, hoping to find refuge, and Twain delivers a sharply observed description of what his hero sees when he is taken in: "It was a mighty nice family, and a mighty nice house, too." In the first sentence of the description, Twain is setting the reader up for a contrast between the appearance of the house ("nice"), and what it represents. Huck continues in his unique vernacular: "On the table in the middle of the room was a kind of lovely crockery basket that had apples and oranges and peaches and grapes piled up in it, which was much redder and yellower and prettier than real ones is, but they warn't real because you could see where pieces had got chipped off and showed the white chalk, or whatever it was, underneath."[2]

Although the log house may not qualify as architecture in the academic sense, Twain in a few words conveys a feeling not only for a building's interior, but also for what it represents. The "crockery basket" is a symbol of the aspirations of a humble family to some level of social status, but it "warn't real," and the pieces that had been chipped off confirm its artificiality. The larger use of the symbol is to reinforce the main theme of Twain's book, that "sivilization," as Huck calls it, is mostly about appearances and hypocrisy, not fundamental human values. Twain makes his point through fictional description, but it is not so different in spirit from Adolf Loos's indictment of tattoos and ornament as signs of social and aesthetic decay in nineteenth-century Vienna.

While Twain's social commentary brings smiles to most faces, the more caustic analysis of American pretensions by F. Scott Fitzgerald provokes a tighter expression. When Nick Carraway first visits Tom and Daisy Buchanan's house in *The Great Gatsby*, the author sets both the scene and the tone for the rest of the book with lean efficiency: "Their house was even more elaborate than I expected, a cheerful red and white Georgian Colonial mansion overlooking the bay." The danger signal is the word *cheerful*, which Fitzgerald uses to alert his readers that the activities in the house are likely to be anything but. Nick continues:

> *The lawn started at the beach and ran toward the front door for a quarter of a mile, jumping over sun dials and brick walls and burning gardens—finally when it reached the house drifting up the side in bright vines as though from the momentum of its run. The front was broken by a line of French windows, glowing now with reflected gold, and wide open to the warm windy afternoon, and Tom Buchanan in riding clothes was standing with his legs apart on the front porch.*[3]

The Buchanan mansion may seem at first to represent dynastic self-assurance, but Fitzgerald has infiltrated his description with details chosen to cast doubt on its authenticity. A lawn that stretches for a quarter of a mile is perhaps too much lawn; sundials are often the garden ornaments of *arrivistes*; French windows are not normally part of Georgian Colonial design. With these details, Fitzgerald is subtly reminding the reader that Tom Buchanan's house and grounds have been cobbled together to convey an impression of old money but do not reflect the hereditary legitimacy that the owner seeks.

Twain and Fitzgerald used their architectural settings to criticize American cultural values. By contrast, Ayn Rand, the libertarian founder of Objectivism, a philosophy celebrating individualism, employed her descriptive powers to advance her views on the virtues of independent thought and action. Here, in her novel *The Fountainhead* (1943), Rand describes the house designed by her main character, the architect Howard Roark: "The Wynand house stood on the hill above them. The earth spread out in terraced fields and rose gradually to make the elevation of the hill. The house was a shape of horizontal rectangles rising toward a slashing vertical projection; a group of diminishing setbacks, each a separate room, its size and form making the successive steps in a series of interlocking floor lines."[4]

With the phrase *slashing vertical projection*, Rand is

acknowledging the architect's masculine power, not to mention her own admiration of it. The author continues:

> *It was as if from the wide living room on the first level a hand had moved slowly, shaping the next steps by a sustained touch, then had stopped, had continued in separate movements, each shorter, brusquer. And had ended, torn off, remaining somewhere in the sky. So that it seemed as if the slow rhythm of the rising fields had been picked up, stressed, accelerated and broken into the staccato chords of the finale.*[5]

The audience for the view includes "Dominique sitting straight, her body rising stiffly from the pale blue circle of her skirt on the grass."[6] It does not take much reading in Sigmund Freud to detect Rand's fascination with sexual domination in her erotic description of Howard Roark's building.

A more nuanced use of architectural description is represented by Evelyn Waugh. His *Brideshead Revisited*, published a year after *The Fountainhead*, chronicles the fading fortunes and tangled relationships of an aristocratic English family. Unlike the Buchanan house, the family seat of the Marchmains is a shrine to old money. Waugh's narrator, Charles Ryder, says of the house:

> *It was an aesthetic education to live within those walls, to wander from room to room, from the Soanesque library to the Chinese drawing-room, adazzle with gilt pagodas and nodding mandarins, painted paper and Chippendale fret-work, from the Pompeian parlour to the great tapestry-hung hall which stood unchanged, as it had been designed two hundred and fifty years before; to sit, hour after hour, in the pillared shade looking out on the terrace.*[7]

Waugh's alliteration—the "pagodas," "painted paper," the "Pompeian parlour," and the "pillared shade"—lulls the reader into the languor of a class whose members had never had to work for a living and expected their inherited good fortune to continue indefinitely.

Charles's description continues as he inspects the basement with his friend Sebastian, the family's dissipated son, and a servant:

> *One day we went down to the cellars with Wilcox and saw the empty bays which had once held a vast store of wine; one transept only was used now; there the bins were well stocked, some of them with vintages fifty years old. "There's*

been nothing added since his Lordship went abroad," said
Wilcox. "A lot of the old wine wants drinking up. We
ought to have laid down the eighteens and twenties. I've
had several letters about it from the wine merchants, but
her Ladyship says to ask Lord Brideshead, and he says to
ask his Lordship, and his Lordship says to ask the lawyers.
That's how we get low. There's enough here for ten years at
the rate it's going, but how shall we be then?"[8]

In this brief but elegant passage about an undistin-
guished subterranean space, one can grasp the slow but
inexorable decline of the entire British Empire!

Evocative description is a fundamental tool of the fiction writer, but it also plays a role in literary nonfiction.
Recalling some of the scholars mentioned in the last
chapter, Mary McCarthy, in her 1956 work *The Stones
of Florence*, provides an eloquent appreciation of one
of the greatest Renaissance architects. Writing about
Filippo Brunelleschi's major monument, the dome of
the cathedral in Florence, she notes that it

is stumbled on like an irreducible fact in the midst of
shops, pasticcerie, and a wild cat's cradle of motor traffic.
It startles by its size and also by its gaiety—the spread

of its flouncing apse and tribune in their Tuscan marble
dress, dark green from Prato, pure white from Carrara,
pink from the Maremma. It is like a mountain but it is
also like a bellying circus tent or festive marquee.[9]

McCarthy's physical description of the surprise that greets a visitor coming upon the Duomo in the tangle of city streets is arresting and immediate, but she takes her analysis to another, more abstract level. She argues that Brunelleschi's architecture

is a species of wisdom, like Socratic and Platonic
philosophy, in which forms are realized in their absolute
integrity and essence; the squareness of square, the
slenderness of slender, the roundness of round. A window,
say, cut out by Brunelleschi is, if that can be conceived,
a Platonic idea of a window: not any particular window
or the sum of existing windows in the aggregate but the
eternal model itself.[10]

No scholar (except perhaps Vincent Scully) would be permitted such poetic flights of interpretation, but McCarthy was a creative writer, and the mission of a creative writer is to engage our feelings as well as our intellects. In this passage, the author—by linking the

Florentine architect to the ancient philosophers—actually manages to do both.

Ross King approaches the same material in an entirely different way. In his *Brunelleschi's Dome*, published in 2000, King concentrates less on the architect's macrocosmic importance than on the microcosmic details that show how his Florentine landmark was executed. Chronicling an average day in the life of the construction workers, King writes:

> Besides their tools, the men also carried their food with them in leather pouches. The noon meal, the comesto, was taken at eleven o'clock, when the church bells sounded a second time. We know that the comesto was normally eaten aloft because in 1426, in order to foil idlers, the Opera decreed that no mason could descend from the dome during the day. This must have meant that even on the hottest summer days the workers did not enjoy their dolce far niente, "sweet idleness," the afternoon siesta when all labors would usually cease because of the scorching temperatures. It was also in 1426 that, on Filippo's orders, a cookshop was installed between the two shells of the cupola in order to serve a noon meal to the workers. The dangers of an open fire on the dome were possibly mitigated

by the fact that the masons also served as Florence's firemen. This responsibility fell to them because they owned the tools used to combat fires in the only way that was practical: tearing down walls to create firebreaks.[11]

Although the details King has selected appear to be mundane, they actually enhance our understanding of how radically innovative Brunelleschi's structure was. Explaining that the workers were forced to labor through the traditional siesta period highlights the importance of the project and the time pressure under which it was being built. Similarly, the description of the cookshop between the shells of the cupola communicates a sense of the dome's structure, which was unprecedented and remains an engineering marvel.

Perhaps the most powerful detail in King's description of the construction site involves the workers' drinking habits. As King reports,

To slake their thirst on the sweltering summer days the workers drank wine, which they carried in flasks along with their tools and lunches. Strange and inadvisable as a draft of wine might seem under these circumstances, whether diluted or not, wine was a healthier drink than

water, which carried bacteria and therefore disease. And
Florentines placed great faith in the wholesome properties
of wine. Drunk in moderation, it was said to improve the
blood, hasten digestion, calm the intellect, enliven the
spirit, and expel wind. It might also have given a fillip of
courage to men clinging to an inward-curving vault several
hundred feet above the ground.[12]

Although the author might simply have stated precisely in feet and inches how high the workmen were from the floor, his inclusion of the image of them drinking wine in a perilous position drives home the impression of the dome's height as no set of statistics could.

John le Carré is an author who made his name as a masterful teller of tales about Cold War espionage, most famously in *Tinker, Tailor, Soldier, Spy*, a fictionalized version of the saga of Kim Philby, the English aristocrat who nearly destroyed the British secret service. As is appropriate to his characteristic theme of uncertain loyalties, le Carré occupies a gray area between literature and popular fiction. But few other writers in any genre have used physical description to achieve as finely shaded portrayals of ideals gone bad, hopes destroyed, and allies betrayed. In one of his early novels, *A Small Town in Germany,* le Carré tells the story of a disaffected government employee with a troubled past who has stolen files from the British embassy in Bonn, which was then the West German capital. As the story lurches toward its gloomy conclusion, the author employs his hallmark skills at infusing an inanimate scene with emotional malaise: "Passing a hospital, they entered a more sombre road where the older suburb had survived; behind the shaggy conifers and blue-black laurel bushes, leaden spires which once had painted donnish dreams of Weimar stood like lances in a mouldering forest."[13] Where Ross King evoked the size of the Florentine cathedral dome by listing the daily routine and crude equipment of Brunelleschi's workmen, le Carré deploys a succession of resonant adjectives to set the tone for his narrative: "sombre," "shaggy," "leaden," "mouldering."

Clearly, we are not in a happy environment, but the author further darkens the mood by invoking three local works of architecture to frame the scene: "Ahead of them rose the Bundestag [the parliament building], naked, comfortless and uncomforted; a vast motel mourned by its own flags and painted in yellowing milk. At its back, straddled by Kennedy's Bridge and bordered by Beethoven's hall, the brown Rhine pursued its uncertain cultural course."[14]

In a few sentences, le Carré has summed up how the pervasive moral ambiguities of his subject have tainted high art (represented by Beethoven's hall), political idealism (represented by a bridge dedicated to an assassinated American president), and attempts to resolve the legacy of the Second World War through democratic institutions (the "naked, comfortless and uncomforted" Bundestag, which has been reduced to the status of a "motel").

Whatever persuaders, critics, and scholars may be able to teach us about the built world rarely matches the impact on our emotions that creative writers can have when they are allowed to engage their imaginations and ours.

Unfortunately, most architecture students and practitioners have limited opportunities to savor such literary pleasures. Most of their days (and nights) must be devoted to convincing teachers, critics, and potential clients of their personal talents and qualifications. This process starts with the way they present themselves to others, and that most often happens through visual images of their own work. But to be most effective, those images must be supported by the skillful use of the written word.

PRESENTATION

No matter how talented architecture students or architects may be, their gifts are not much use if no one else knows about them. A vital step toward success is to present oneself to others in the most favorable and accessible way. But no amount of snappy graphics can compensate for a weak or inappropriate written message.

GUGGENHEIM MUSEUM BILBAO
BILBAO, SPAIN
FRANK GEHRY

SEVEN

PRESENTATION
Showing Your Stuff

NO MATTER HOW TALENTED architecture students or architects may be, their gifts are not of much use if no one else knows about them. So a vital step toward success is to present oneself to others in the most favorable and accessible way. In school, that means excelling at assignments and creating a strong portfolio to get the best grades and recommendations. Once out in the marketplace, however, presenting one's work to the public is a matter of professional survival.

This is a complex undertaking. For one thing, some architects are still handicapped by feelings that self-promotion is somehow beneath their dignity. In decades past, most leading American architects were graduates of a few eastern schools, traveled in interlocking social circles, and often had independent incomes. In those days, such gentleman designers (there were almost no women) could expect to rely for commissions on referrals from family, friends, or club mates. No more. Indeed, many prominent architecture firms now have entire departments dedicated to promoting their services to potential clients.

However, for architects who are just starting out, or for small firms, the first step is usually some form of printed mission statement or brochure. High-quality paper, a legible typeface, and an attractive design are important, but no amount of snappy graphics can compensate for a weak or inappropriate written message. And the best messages conform to the structural principles we have been examining from the beginning of this book.

All architecture schools encourage their students to be creative and may even urge them to defy conventional thinking. But the general public is rarely sympathetic to what is called "discourse" in university design studios, where students can get away with terms like *entangentality, morphogenetic,* and *performicity.* It can be hazardous to use the same sort of approach in a publication to communicate to the outside world. The firm of Diller Scofidio + Renfro is now well established, having designed the Museum of Contemporary Art in Boston and the much-praised addition to Alice Tully Hall at New York's Lincoln Center. But their professional start was probably delayed by the description of their services they circulated when they were making their debut in the early 1980s: "The work of Diller + Scofidio is situated between 'inscription' and 'prescription' and architecture of 'description' concerned with the hyper-present." This sort of posturing lingo is likely to appeal only to architecture insiders, not to boards of directors who are being asked to invest millions of dollars in a design.

The founder of a small architecture firm in Connecticut discovered the hazards of inappropriate messaging when he and his wife opened an office shortly after they graduated from architecture school. The mission statement they sent to several likely clients began: "Building is a radical act." As an invitation, the sentence was certain to attract readers' attention but not necessarily instill confidence. The architect reported a few years later that, after several months during which "the phones were not ringing," he and his wife revised their letter. The new one began: "All good architecture begins with the client." From then on, their practice grew steadily.

A more focused statement can be found in the profile of a twenty-person office, this one specializing in designs for schools, community organizations, and recreational facilities. The text reads: "The [firm's] hallmark solution balances innovative design, natural setting, organizational context and the considerations of future generations." Although design is an obvious and essential ingredient, the phrases *natural setting* and *future generations* are certain to appeal to heads of schools and directors of recreational facilities. This statement is specific, unpretentious, and admirably brief.

The Atlanta firm of Mack Scogin Merrill Elam Architects uses its print profile to address a common concern among many clients who retain nationally known architects—that their projects will be relegated to junior members of the firm. In their first paragraph, the architects write that the partners "have made the commitment to organize all of the work in a manner that ensures their involvement in the day-to-day development of each project. This keeps the work personal and directed, and brings the best of the firm's collective knowledge and experience to each project."

The difficulty of presenting one's virtues to the public is not limited to small and medium-size firms. A partner in one of the country's most prominent high-rise design offices confessed to my architecture school class that he and his partners used to meet every year to review their written materials, and that "every year they got worse." An excerpt from one version read: "Our aspiration within a global context is to evolve a form of architectural alchemy with the fusion of our culture and another. Hopefully this fusion offers the possibility to bring about something new and meaningful, to both and from both. Solutions emerge that could not be achieved without the interaction of both cultures." One can easily imagine each partner earnestly lobbying for word changes with the best of intentions, only to produce a murky statement that says very little. Even at the highest levels, clarity remains the key to communication.

No architect can expect to communicate these days

through print alone. Increasingly, the most important medium is the Web. It has almost replaced print in some quarters, and while architects developing websites must still observe the principles of good organization and clear expression, they must apply them under different constraints. A recent study by Microsoft revealed that "the first ten seconds of the page visit are critical for users' decision to stay or leave" and that the average page visit lasts less than a minute. If this reminds you of your high school guidance counselor's advice about writing your college application essay, it should. The stakes are high, and you have very little space in which to make a good impression. (The lengths of an average Web page and the main essay on the Common Application are similar, between 250 and 650 words.) Moreover, according to the Microsoft study, Web viewers rarely read more than about one-quarter of the text. The researchers' conclusion: "Unless your writing is extraordinarily clear and focused, little of what you say on your website will get through to customers."[1] An article on architecture firm websites in *Architectural Record* endorsed that view: "Websites are a vital marketing tool.

Unless you're a superstar design firm, steer clear of archispeak and tricky graphics. Users want a site that is clean and simple."[2]

A brief review of websites produced by some leading architecture firms reveals a surprising range of awareness about this relatively new medium. The avant-garde Dutch firm OMA, led by Rem Koolhaas, declares in the opening sentence of its site that, in addition to architecture and urbanism, it specializes in "cultural analysis." This may appeal to intellectual clients, but perhaps not to the more pragmatically minded. The Los Angeles–based office Morphosis, whose founder Thom Mayne, like Koolhaas, is known for innovative design, presents the Web visitor with a bold set of banner lines that includes "architecture," "urban design," "research," and "media," but also "tangents & outtakes." To the architecturally initiated, the last two terms may have strong appeal, but they may also test a more conventional client's confidence.

Consistent with her profile as an international celebrity, Zaha Hadid pushes the limits of Web prose. The "About Us" section of her firm's page contains this declaration: "We create transformative cultural, corporate, residential and other spaces that work in synchronicity with their surroundings." The word *synchronicity* may impress a reader with Hadid's aspirations. However, the psychologist Carl Jung, who originated the concept, defined it as a meaningful connection between apparently unrelated events: coincidences that were "meant to happen." How this relates to architecture is hard to establish, and asking potential clients to think through the connection in a ten-second visit may send them to another website and another architect.

Since Frank Gehry is widely credited with helping to transform recent architecture from the rectilinear to the sculptural, it is interesting to note how matter-of-fact his website language is in comparison with that of Koolhaas, Mayne, and Hadid. Although Gehry's page is illustrated with what looks like a scribble (actually a hand-drawn sketch for one of the architect's museums), the first sentence leaves no room for Hadidian confusion. "Frank Gehry Partners, LLP," it declares, "is a full service firm with broad international experience in academic, commercial, museum, performance, and residential projects." The text goes on to note that the firm has a staff of more than 250 but that "every project undertaken by Gehry Partners is designed personally and directly by Frank Gehry" using "a sophisticated 3D computer modeling program originally created for use by the aerospace industry." In three tight statements, Gehry (1) informs potential clients of the firm's comprehensive reach, (2) reassures those who might worry about being given minimal attention by the firm's star, and (3) anchors his creative process in the most advanced technology. Whatever one may think of Gehry's free-form aesthetic, his Web presentation could not be more down-to-earth.

While websites are useful in providing gateways to architects, they are not necessarily the best way to provide more detailed information about a firm's work. For that, many architects still turn to ink-on-paper monographs. These books, which are usually elaborately designed and richly illustrated, can be enormously expensive; they are almost always paid for by the firm rather than by a commercial publisher. However, they are both more tangible and more durable than websites, and they can have substantial long-term impact, especially if given to clients or displayed on coffee tables in board rooms and country mansions where potential customers may see them.

The design of any monograph should reflect the firm's aesthetic, but not to excess. Some firms that attempt to create a "hot" look can end up with an artistic statement that conveys little useful information and can actually deter a reader. (Tiny gray type on a white page may win graphic design prizes, but is hard for the mature eyes of most clients to read. The same applies to websites.) Similarly, the text should reflect the firm's philosophy in a positive light, without seeming too self-congratulatory. To do that, many leading firms hire established authors to contribute introductions or appreciations. A number of architecture critics have created something of a cottage industry writing introductions to volumes on such major designers as Renzo Piano, Kohn Pedersen Fox, and Cesar Pelli. Some firms prefer to give their books a more scholarly flavor, and select their commentators accordingly. The historian Joseph Rykwert wrote the main essay for a 1984 Rizzoli monograph on Richard Meier;

Jean-Louis Cohen, of NYU's Institute of Fine Arts, contributed to the 2001 volume on Frank Gehry published
by the Guggenheim Museum; and Yale's Vincent Scully
has lent a scholarly dimension to several monographs
on Robert A. M. Stern.

Like a convincing work of scholarship, a good monograph should allow readers to come to their own conclusions about a firm's qualifications. One temptation is
to attempt to be all things to all potential clients. A few
major firms, such as Gensler or Skidmore, Owings &
Merrill, may be able to span the entire design spectrum.
Gensler's website says its projects "can be as small as a
wine label or as large as a new urban district," but some
of the most successful offices have prospered by tightly
defining their specialties and limiting their commissions. An example is William Rawn Associates. This
Boston office with a staff of thirty-five placed first in
Architect magazine's national ranking of firms based
on "profitability, sustainable ethos, and design quality."
The Rawn firm beat out larger organizations by concen-
trating on a limited range of buildings—mostly institutional, cultural, and educational—and turning away

commissions rather than expanding beyond what the partners considered their capabilities; as their brochure explains, Rawn "has only five projects in active design at any one time."

Architecture firms can control what they build, but they cannot control the reaction to it. Dealing with the media is a crucial component of professional success. Professional public relations (PR) firms can be helpful, but many critics and other writers on architecture dismiss PR releases as unreliable because they are usually transparently self-serving. Since architectural journalists tend to be territorial about their knowledge of the field, there are few things as annoying to them as overly aggressive PR people who insist that they know better. Nevertheless, it is a good idea to make sure that influential writers know about important projects and awards, and if that can be done in an indirect way through personal contacts or a graceful letter, the journalist may adopt the idea as his or her own discovery. The architecture and urban planning firm of Cooper, Robertson & Partners regularly sends out postcards of their work accompanied by a personal note from one of the principals.

Where you get covered is important. While a glowing article in an industry trade journal such as *Engineering News Record* or *Building Stone Magazine* is certainly worth having, even a small mention in the *Wall Street Journal*, the *Dallas Morning News*, or the *Los Angeles Times* is usually more valuable. As in the case of criticism and scholarship, the reason is that readers tend to trust publications with a reputation for independence and credibility over publications that serve an obvious agenda.

Should you get a favorable notice in *any* publication, a letter of appreciation to the writer or the editor can have lasting effects. Few journalists consider themselves overpaid, and an old-fashioned thank-you note—as long as it is not sycophantic—is always welcome added compensation. Nowadays, something handwritten is so rare that it can have added impact. (Former US president George H. W. Bush softened many political skeptics by sending them handwritten personal letters.) Make sure the note is literate, even if it is in electronic form. Sending something that is clumsily worded and has grammatical or spelling errors is no way to impress someone with your professionalism. One partner in a prominent architecture firm that specializes in school and university buildings routinely circulates job applicants' letters that include *it's* as a possessive or substitutes *their* for *there* to remind his own staff of the stakes involved. On the other hand, it is hard for a critic to think ill of an architect who writes: "I just read your piece in *ArtNews*. It is thoughtful, perceptive, knowledgeable, well written and generous," or one who simply says, "Bravo!"

The traditional architectural press is shrinking, and in any case it is not always read by potential clients. So-called shelter magazines—such as *Better Homes and Gardens, Southern Living,* and *Sunset*—provide alternative routes to the public. One architect who had approached the established professional publications for years with little success eventually turned to *Architectural Digest*. The glossy monthly has never been considered a source of critical analysis, but it is read by wealthy people, and the architect thought he might catch the attention of some who might be interested in building elaborate houses. He was right, and landed a substantial commission for a country house.

Even more effective than being published is establishing bonds with people who make decisions, both financial and aesthetic. Those bonds often start with a letter of introduction. The letter might begin with a sentence that shows an awareness of the client's sensibilities and preferences, like this one sent to the head of a religious organization. It read: "I have long admired the way in which your buildings have combined an attention to spirituality with a sensitivity to design. Although I realize that there may be nothing on your calendar at the moment, I hope you won't mind my introducing the work of our firm through the enclosed images of a recent chapel and some responses to it in the architectural press." James Gamble Rogers became the house architect of Yale University in the 1920s and 1930s through his association with the Harkness family, who were patrons of several campus buildings, and Ralph Adams Cram developed a similar relationship with Princeton. More recently, I. M. Pei's friendship with Paul Mellon carried the architect from the commission for a small art building at a New England boarding school to the East Building of the National Gallery. Frank Gehry's connection with Thomas Krens, the former director of the Guggenheim Museum, has borne fruit well beyond Bilbao. These clients did not find their architects in the Yellow Pages, but even when a personal recommendation is involved, literate and informative correspondence often serves as a test of a firm's institutional and personal fit.

Sometimes, however, a too-aggressive overture can backfire. A prominent New York City real estate developer made a practice of romancing critics about the achievements of his architects with a force that verged on the threatening. When reviews were not to his liking, he was quick to retaliate, once calling the editor of a magazine to denounce its critic in a shower of expletives. One prominent high-design architect could be charming when showing critics his designs or conducting a tour of a construction site, but when he suffered almost universally negative criticism for his addition to a beloved modern landmark, he lost a great deal of potential support by sending abusive notes to writers who found fault with his design.

A well-worded invitation to review a firm's portfolio or even see a design in its early stage is not always interpreted as an attempt at seduction. And even temporarily unhappy relationships can often be repaired with positive long-term results. A partner in Skidmore, Owings & Merrill who had been criticized in a magazine review for one of his buildings disarmed the writer by conceding in a personal note that the critic at least "had a point." And Cesar Pelli, whose 1990 addition to Carnegie Hall drew critical fire in some quarters, ensured future sympathy from one local critic by sending a handwritten letter that explained the constraints under which he had been working, adding, "Let's have lunch."

PROFESSIONAL COMMUNICATION

Good writers provide readers with what they need: an invitation; an explanation of the importance of the material; enough history to prepare the readers to understand the writer's point; a detailed development of the core argument; a summary of the main points; a suggestion about where the future lies; and a conclusion that reminds the readers of where they began and leaves them with a provocative thought.

PHILLIPS EXETER ACADEMY LIBRARY
EXETER, NEW HAMPSHIRE
LOUIS KAHN

EIGHT

PROFESSIONAL COMMUNICATION
Getting the Job

THERE ARE SCORES of memorable aphorisms involving architecture, ranging from Daniel Burnham's "Make no little plans," to Ludwig Mies van der Rohe's "Less is more," to Robert Venturi's "Less is a bore." But surely the most practical is attributed to Henry Hobson Richardson, who is said to have declared, "The first rule of architecture is to get the job." There is no fixed set of procedures for following Richardson's advice, but some practices are considered basic, and they must include good writing.

Most often, the process begins with a request from a client for an architect's qualifications, or RFQ, followed by RFPs, or requests for proposals. One letter of invitation, for an urban science center, began this way: "We are soliciting interest from architects who have sustained, documented records of design excellence and international peer recognition." It went on to describe the project: "Our new facility will be a bold, striking building that is welcoming to patrons and inviting to passersby." The client's charge was "to inspire lifelong learning through interactive and innovative experiences that explore our changing world through science." In addition to a functional and distinctive building, the client called for one that would have a role beyond its immediate purpose: "This highly visible site will serve as a gateway into the city. It will also be an integral component in the rejuvenation of the city's downtown."

A key to responding to RFQs and RFPs is learning as much as possible about both the project and the client. Has the client done similar projects before? Were they successful? What are the comparable buildings by other architects—past and present—that would make points of reference for a proposal? Does the client have a reputation for working well with architects, and—very important—paying bills on time? Has the client been involved in any legal actions? Is the client an individual with the authority to make decisions, or a committee whose members must be dealt with as a group or separately? With the answers to these questions, a firm can develop a strategy for competing for the commission. This can include interviews with principals, formal group meetings with consultants who might collaborate on the commission, visual presentations, and even golf outings, but the process usually begins with a letter.

In my architecture school class, we practice for the process by imagining that the students are members of a firm competing for a job. (This is like the exercise in chapter 1 of making up an academic paper before starting on the research; it helps the writer and the architect to generate as many ideas as possible that may be relevant to the assignment.) The actual building is selected from suggestions proposed by the students, and over the years the buildings have included a community center, a university library, an inner-city grocery store, a mixed-use commercial high-rise, and a regional transportation hub.

One of the most interesting of these imaginary commissions was a public library for the downtown area of an economically depressed city. The first step in the process was to assess the scope of the project compared with the capabilities of the firm. For the purposes of the exercise, we assumed that our firm had already designed two libraries—one for a private university, the other for a city like the one issuing our imaginary RFP. We also discussed how we might engage the client in a discussion about the larger historical and cultural roles of libraries by reviewing the special qualities of such buildings as Richardson's intimate 1882 Crane Library in Quincy, Massachusetts; McKim, Mead & White's majestic 1895 Boston Public Library and its 1973 addition by Philip Johnson and John Burgee; and Louis Kahn's austere 1971 building for the Phillips Exeter Academy in New Hampshire. The students felt that these references would allow them to demonstrate to the client their depth of knowledge about the building type, and to do so in a way that went beyond the specifics of the program.

While it is best to have experience in the specific building type required by the client, architects may be able to benefit from its lack by emphasizing the advantages of taking a fresh approach. A partner in a medium-sized and highly successful firm specializing in institutional work told me that he had found that certain clients are attracted to architects with proven credentials who are willing to take on a new challenge that might produce creative ways of handling familiar material. In the case of a library—a building type that is being reinvented in response to changing technology—the opportunity to emphasize the advantages of an unorthodox design would be especially attractive.

The second step in the class exercise was to investigate the goals and aspirations of the people making the hiring decision. Again, for the purposes of the exercise, the students established that the client was a committee made up of school board members, teachers, and businesspeople who would be helping to raise money. Knowing about a client's background, education, and professional associations can often create a personal bond (and occasionally prevent inadvertent missteps, such as joking about a championship football game that went against the client's college).

The letter the students wrote for the library competition adhered to our familiar structural principles. It began: "We all are familiar with the traditional image of a public library: books, magazines, reading rooms with green lampshades, leather chairs, and wood panelling. We are also highly aware that this image has been changing rapidly and radically. The first agent of this change is digitization." You should be able to identify the type of opening the students used: a variation on the basic then-and-now.

The next paragraph also fit our established pattern, moving quickly to the reason the client should read on: "In the case of your library, an equally important consideration is the evolving demographics of your neighborhood. Gentrification, ethnic diversity, and growing numbers of families with young children all require an expanded definition of the traditional library." The students composed two versions of the section discussing the firm's qualifications in the field of library design. One referred to the two libraries they had already designed; the other conceded that libraries were a new field for them, but argued that their openness to new ideas about libraries would produce an original result. The students then developed this core statement: "We are particularly interested in a library that fosters not only the exchange of information through advanced technology, but also promotes a greater sense of community." As in the case of our examples in persuasion, criticism, and scholarship, this sentence established the importance of the argument and encouraged the readers to keep reading.

The next paragraph reminded the client that the firm had a documented record of honoring schedules and meeting budgets—matters that are absolutely fundamental to the financial members of any selection committee. The students concluded with a gesture toward the future of the institution and its surroundings: "We appreciate the need to anticipate still further changes as the city and your institution grow." Even with limited prompting from the instructor, the students' letter turned out to be remarkably similar to ones written by several successful professional firms, and considerably better than many real ones in my files.

The students' use of the word *community* is important in this setting, because it was intended to let the reader know that the architects were concerned with satisfying more than the basic requirements of the program. We have discussed in previous chapters the impact of word choice in writing. Unsubstantiated claims by a critic that a building is breathtaking, absurd, or historic make thoughtful readers wonder whether they can trust the writer. We have seen that a similar problem of credibility applies to scholars who assert their feelings at the expense of documentation. In competing for a commission, architects need to observe some of the same caution, but in this case a measure of unsupported enthusiasm can actually add to the firm's appeal. A letter to a client who was considering a new arts complex on a university campus provides a good example. In the first paragraph, the architects declared that they intended to create a "transformative place" that would establish for the institution "a distinctive position in education through the arts." They predicted that their plan would result in "a bold and dynamic" complex of "iconic buildings" contributing to a "cross-disciplinary laboratory" that would provide a "catalyst" in "nurturing spontaneity." While there was no way to prove they could deliver all this, the language conveys a sense that the architects saw the project as a mission. It could only impress the client that the applicants had vision as well as competence.

In addition to the main RFQ or RFP response letter, supporting documents may be helpful, as long as they do not overwhelm the clients with more information than is needed to secure their interest. Presentation books can be powerful tools in documenting a firm's design experience and special qualifications for the assignment. One such book included a detailed description showing how the firm creates a self-contained studio within the larger organization that is devoted exclusively to the design of each project. Others document past projects and their performance, as well as the specialized consultants who may have participated in the design.

However, most architecture firms are not able to produce such lavish publications. A partner in a more modest office told me that one of his simplest—and most effective—documents was a single sheet of paper. His firm specializes in the design of suburban country clubs. The document was a chart listing the forty-six clubs for which the firm had previously worked, and it included seven columns—one each for specific program requirements such as "main clubhouse," "golf shop," and "turf maintenance." Each column was marked with a red dot if the firm had provided the service in the past, and the columns were thick with red dots. Although not a work of fine prose, the sheet provided at a glance a comprehensive record of the firm's expertise, and convincingly supplemented the letter expressing the firm's interest in the commission. According to the firm's founding partner, the chart was described by one client as the single most persuasive document in the decision to hire the architect.

No matter how much work a firm may have done in a specific field, potential clients want to know which members will be doing the work on their job and what qualifications they have. In our class exercise, the students created an imaginary résumé for each of their partners and selected the ones who seemed most appropriate to the project. This is routine in professional practice, but it should not be taken lightly. The way you present the qualifications of your staff can either give the client confidence or create barriers. In the written biographies that usually accompany RFQ responses, a heavy sprinkling of degrees from prominent liberal arts schools may reassure clients with similar educational backgrounds, but might intimidate those with more technical credentials. On the other hand, too heavy an emphasis on technological skills might suggest a lack of creativity. In any case, many firms make a point of employing and listing architects who also hold degrees in law, business, and environmental regulation, areas that are likely to reassure clients who may be worried about an *excess* of creativity in an era of shrinking budgets and increasing litigation.

A corollary to the presentation of professional credentials is a reminder to clients that their voices will be heard in the creative process, not drowned out by a design diva. One major firm with international reach was careful to include in its letter to a client this sentence: "We are committed to designing buildings which are unique to their region and context and are not constrained by a personal style or signature." Of course, if the client is looking for a famous designer such as Zaha Hadid or Frank Gehry to put on the building's letterhead (or door, as in "New York by Gehry," a 2012 residential high-rise in lower Manhattan otherwise known as 8 Spruce Street), this caution does not apply.

The classroom exercises were validated—and can be summarized—by the experience of a rural arts organization that was planning an addition to a much-loved tranquil retreat for research and a social gathering place. It could not integrate those functions with computers and other new technology. As the RFP put it: "Over time, the building's program has expanded, as new functions have been superimposed on a finite space." The organization needed an addition that would provide access to "creative work in all media."

The list of contending architects ranged from emerging firms to ones with international reputations. Competence was never an issue. According to members of the selection committee, the most important qualification was that the architect should understand and embrace the mission of the institution, which was to nurture the development of original art. The architects who eventually won the commission took this charge seriously, doing extended research into the history of the institution and spending several days on the property, meeting informally with members of the staff and with the artists in residence. In their cover letter to the committee—which ran to only four paragraphs—the architects invoked the creative interactions among artists who had previously attended the institution, writing: "One conversation in particular, between two Nebraskans, encapsulates the importance of having individual as well as shared space." They then quoted from a work by one of those artists, who had written: "The important thing is that the book be written, the picture be painted, the symphony burst forth, the song sing its way into life from the heart of the artist."

According to a member of the selection committee, the architects' demonstrated willingness to dig into the institution's history, spend time on its grounds, meet with its people, and identify a relevant quotation from a former resident immediately moved them to the short list. But other contenders showed similar creativity. What sealed the decision was an early and candid statement by the first team about its approach to money. They wrote: "Because of our strong desire to work with you on this important project, we invite further discussion to clarify and review any questions you may have about the fee proposal or the assumptions we have made. Only through dialogue do we produce our best work." This elegantly direct statement made clear to the committee that the architects—whose artistic credentials were not in doubt—understood finances and that they were willing to work collaboratively. Subsequent letters included a few grammatical errors. One board member found this charming and argued that it was evidence of art triumphing over regulations. No prudent architect should count on such sympathy; more often, the impression given by minor mistakes in writing is of incompetence in large matters as well as small. Happily for the architects, the hiring decision had already been made.

If all this sounds similar to the structural principles discussed in earlier chapters, it should. Whether the product is an academic paper, a work of criticism, or a work of scholarship, a competent writer on architecture needs to provide readers with what they need: an *invitation*; an explanation of the *importance* of the material sufficient to keep the readers reading; enough *history* to prepare the readers to understand the writer's point; a detailed *development* of the core argument; a *summary* of the main points; a suggestion about where the *future* of the subject lies; and a *conclusion* that reminds the readers where they began and leaves them with a provocative thought for reflection. The author of a response to an RFQ or an RFP needs to anticipate all the questions that clients might raise in reading it, then organize a written presentation in an accessible format. Overstating one's qualifications, underestimating the project's scope, confusing the reader with irrelevant information—and writing badly—are sure to raise doubts in readers' minds about an architect's competence. Even if a written proposal is candid, objective, organized, and creative, its authors may not always get the job, but if it fails in any of those areas, they are almost sure to lose it.

CONCLUSION

Few of us can be called brilliant at what we do, but most of us can achieve a high level of competence if we pay attention to the basics. Even for talented writers, a reliable structure is basic to making good results more predictable than accidental. If they do that well, the architecture they advocate may take tangible shape as the lasting artifacts of our own civilization.

LOUVRE PYRAMID
PARIS, FRANCE
I. M. PEI

CONCLUSION

The Writer's Role in Architecture

WHILE BUILDINGS MIGHT seem to speak for themselves, even the best ones may need some help to be fully appreciated. That help often takes the form of writing that explains the issues raised by those buildings, "translating" information that may not at first be apparent. Do they fulfill their clients' goals? Are they appropriate to their sites? Are they aesthetically pleasing? By what standards? In answering these questions, the writer can be architecture's most powerful advocate.

This book is meant to help that writer make the greatest possible impact. Its origins go back to my elementary school years. My father was a writer, and when I showed little talent for numbers, he urged me to stick to words. I did, but in college and graduate school I concentrated in architectural history, and was determined that at some point I would write about the subject.

Fortunately, however, I served an apprenticeship in journalism, starting at the Associated Press (AP). The AP, founded in 1846 and long known as "the by-line of dependability," remains a bedrock institution, one that provides news to thousands of print publications and electronic information outlets around the world. While the distribution of information has changed radically during the AP's history, the goals of its reporting remain, as one of my editors memorably insisted, to be "light, tight, and right," standards against which I still check my own prose.

From the AP, I moved on to a newsmagazine, which allowed me a much wider range of writing than quick summaries of news about bus crashes and bridge collapses. Some forms of magazine writing came easily to me, but I had never asked myself why I knew how to do what I did. The answer was that I didn't.

Many years ago, someone told me about what happened to a centipede when asked which of his hundred feet he put down in what sequence. Since he had never thought about the matter, he ended up paralyzed by confusion. Like the centipede, most people have never thought about why or how they do things that seem to come naturally. Few of us can be called brilliant at what we do, but most of us can achieve a high level of competence if we pay attention to the basics. And even for those who are talented writers, a reliable structure—knowing which feet come down when—is basic to making good results more predictable than accidental.

This was driven home to me early in my career as a writer. My easy way with feature stories on the arts and education foundered on more hard-core assignments about politics and economics. My copy was so heavily revised that a sympathetic editor finally took me aside and explained that there was a system to writing clearly, regardless of the topic. He laid out for me the bare bones of the approach I have described in this book. Gradually, everything began to make sense: I knew which foot went down first!

I was able to take that knowledge with me when I later began writing about architecture professionally as a critic. I know it helped me explain to a lay public not only the aesthetic aspects of architecture but also the mysteries of zoning, floor-area ratios, and preservation law. The more I came to know about architecture, however, the more I realized that the people who write about it have a special obligation. While clarity of expression is important to writers in any profession, those who practice or promote architecture face a unique challenge. At best, they operate at the highest levels of artistic inspiration, but if they are to see that inspiration in built form, they must express themselves in a way that is accessible to the clients who will finance and execute their designs. Because of this need to function in such disparate realms, the ability to communicate in writing is perhaps more important for architects than it might be for other professionals.

The previous chapters are intended to focus the attention of those who write about architecture and its related fields on the richness of the ways in which it has been done in the past—whether through persuasion, criticism, scholarship, literature, promotion, or professional communication—and provide guidance in how to do it for today's readers. But they are also meant to serve as a reminder that clear communication shares some fundamental organizational components across all genres of architectural writing, from travelogues to business letters, from proposals to promotional brochures, from websites to blogs. These follow the familiar sequence that was introduced to me by my former editor, which is really just a distillation of the way we have been telling each other stories since storytelling began. One must first secure the readers' attention, then persuade them of the importance of what one is writing, then provide sufficient background information so that the readers can follow one's argument. Having done this, the good architecture writer will proceed with a development of the argument, summarize it, suggest how the issues may play out in the future, and, finally, end with a resonant conclusion that leaves readers thinking constructively about the topic.

Those who care about enhancing the place of architecture in our society should not assume that talent for design will carry the day—or land the job. Images can be compelling, but the ideas behind them are often best conveyed through the written word, especially to potential clients and others who may have no visual training and don't know how to read plans or elevations.

Over the centuries, architecture has helped define civilizations by creating their most lasting artifacts. Explaining their importance (and getting them paid for) is increasingly the responsibility of people who know how to put architecture's highest aspirations for built form into written words. If they do that well, those forms will ultimately take tangible shape as the lasting artifacts of our own civilization.

BAUHAUS BUILDING
DESSAU, GERMANY
WALTER GROPIUS

ACKNOWLEDGMENTS

FOR THEIR HELP on this book, I thank Sylvan Barnet, John Belle, Ann Birckmayer, Fred Bland, Karla Britton, Fred Clarke, Gregory Clement, Peter Clement, Joan Davidson, John Fifield, Kurt Forster, Alexander Garvin, Rosalie Genevro, Frances Halsband, Dolores Hayden, Julie Iovine, Robert Ivy, Sean Khorsandi, Robert Kliment, George Knight, Robert MacNeil, Cathleen McGuigan, Dietrich Neumann, Alan Organschi, Cesar Pelli, Alan Plattus, Alexander Purves, Douglas Rae, James Gamble Rogers III, Mark Simon, Robert A. M. Stern, Billie Tsien, David Wilk, and Tod Williams.

I am also grateful to Tom Payton and Sarah Nawrocki of Trinity University Press; to freelance editor Christi Stanforth; to David Peattie and Tanya Grove; to my literary agent, Sterling Lord, for his professionalism, persistence, and faith; to Furthermore, a program of the

J. M. Kaplan Fund, for its support of my work over many years; to the Paul Rudolph Foundation; to my students at the Yale School of Architecture; and to Carol Herselle Krinsky, for her high standards, sharp editorial eye, and great heart.

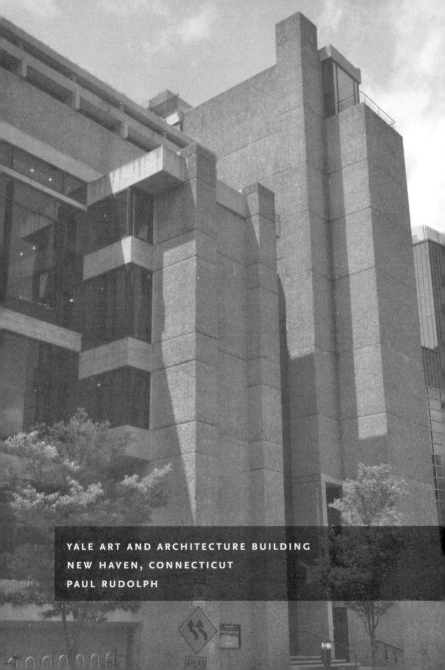

YALE ART AND ARCHITECTURE BUILDING
NEW HAVEN, CONNECTICUT
PAUL RUDOLPH

NOTES

INTRODUCTION

1. Norman Weinstein, "Artful Writing," *Chronicle of Higher Education,* March 7, 2008.

2. Robert Campbell, "Critique," *Architectural Record,* October 2001.

3. Author interview with Robert A. M. Stern, April 1, 2010.

1. STRUCTURE

1. Roger Angell, in *The Elements of Style,* by William Strunk, Jr. and E. B. White (Needham Heights, Mass.: Allyn & Bacon, 2000), foreword, ix.

2. Cathleen McGuigan, "Maverick Master," *Newsweek,* June 17, 1991, 54.

2. STANDARDS

1. Brent Brolin, *The Designer's Eye* (New York: W. W. Norton, 2002).

2. Quoted in *Sidewalk Critic: Lewis Mumford's Writings on New*

York, ed. Robert Wojtowicz (New York: Princeton Architectural Press, 1998), 108.

3. Elliot Willensky and Norval White, *AIA Guide to New York City* (New York: Harcourt Brace Jovanovich, third edition, 1988), 273.

4. Ada Louise Huxtable, "Huntington Hartford's Palatial Midtown Museum," *New York Times,* February 25, 1964.

5. Ada Louise Huxtable, "The Building You Love to Hate," *New York Times,* December 12, 1971.

3. PERSUASION

1. Full text reprinted in *The Architecture Reader,* ed. A. Krista Sykes (New York: Braziller, 2007), 91–93.

2. Full text reprinted in Sykes, *The Architecture Reader,* trans. Michael Mitchell, 103–109.

3. Full text reprinted in *Frank Lloyd Wright Collected Writings,* vol. 1 (1894–1930), ed. Bruce Brooks Pfeiffer (New York: Rizzoli, 1992), 333–336.

4. Ralph Adams Cram, *My Life in Architecture* (Boston: Little, Brown and Company, 1936).

5. Jane Jacobs, *The Death and Life of Great American Cities* (New York: Random House, 1961).

6. Robert Venturi, *Complexity and Contradiction in Architecture* (New York: Museum of Modern Art, 1966).

7. Rem Koolhaas, *Delirious New York, a Retroactive Manifesto for Manhattan* (New York: Oxford University Press, 1978).

4 . CRITICISM

1. Thomas Fisher, "The Death and Life of Great Architecture Criticism," *Places*, December 1, 2011.

2. Alexandra Lange, *Writing about Architecture* (New York: Princeton Architectural Press, 2011), 8.

3. Lewis Mumford, "Machinery and the Modern Style," *New Republic*, August 3, 1921, 263–265.

4. Ada Louise Huxtable, "Pennzoil: Houston's Towering Achievement," *New York Times*, February 22, 1976.

5. Ada Louise Huxtable, "The Best Way to Preserve 2 Columbus Circle," *Wall Street Journal*, January 7, 2004.

6. Paul Goldberger, "The Portland Building," reprinted in *On the Rise: Architecture and Design in a Modern Age* (New York: Times Books, 1983), 161–164.

7. Herbert Muschamp, "Zaha Hadid's Urban Mother Ship," *New York Times*, June 8, 2003.

8. Michael Sorkin, "Critique," *Architectural Record*, August 2004, 63–64.

9. *Boston Globe,* November 14, 2008.

10. Ibid., 268.

11. Peter Blake, *Form Follows Fiasco* (Boston: Little, Brown and Company, 1977), 163.

12. Ibid., 25.

13. Tom Wolfe, *From Bauhaus to Our House* (New York: Farrar, Straus and Giroux, 1981), 17.

14. Ibid., 117.

15. Ibid., 140.

5. SCHOLARSHIP

1. Henry-Russell Hitchcock and Philip Johnson, *The International Style* (1932; rev. ed., New York: W. W. Norton, 1995), 36.

2. Ibid., 13.

3. Ibid., 46.

4. Ibid., 42.

5. Talbot Hamlin, *Architecture through the Ages* (1940; reprint, New York: G. P. Putnam's Sons, 1953), 562.

6. Ibid., 576.

7. Carl W. Condit, *The Chicago School of Architecture* (Chicago: University of Chicago Press, 1964), 128.

8. Ibid., 133.

9. Ibid., 134.

10. Vincent Scully, *Architecture: The Natural and the Manmade* (New York: St. Martin's, 1991), 39.

11. Ibid., 40.

12. Ibid., 5.

13. Ibid., 14.

14. William H. Jordy, *American Buildings and Their Architects: The Impact of European Modernism in the Mid-Twentieth Century* (Garden City, NY: Doubleday & Company, Anchor Books Edition), 87.

15. Ibid., 88.

16. Ibid., 90.

17. Ibid., 163.

18. Ibid.

19. Gwendolyn Wright, *USA* (London: Reaktion Books, 2008), 8.

20. Ibid., 15.

21. Ibid., 24.

22. Ibid., 35.

23. Ibid., 125.

24. Ibid., 260.

25. Ibid., 250.

26. Ibid., 256.

6. LITERATURE

1. Franz Kafka, *The Castle*, trans. Mark Harman (New York: Schocken Books, 1998), 8.

2. Mark Twain, *The Adventures of Huckleberry Finn* (New York: Bantam Books, 1981), 100.

3. F. Scott Fitzgerald, *The Great Gatsby* (New York: Simon & Schuster, 2003), 11.

4. Ayn Rand, *The Fountainhead* (New York: Penguin Books, 1993), 584.

5. Ibid.

6. Ibid.

7. Evelyn Waugh, *Brideshead Revisited* (Boston: Little, Brown, and Company, 1999), 80.

8. Ibid., 83.

9. Mary McCarthy, *The Stones of Florence* (New York: Harcourt, 1963), 130.

10. Ibid., 142.

11. Ross King, *Brunelleschi's Dome* (New York: Penguin Books, 2000), 51.

12. Ibid., 52.

13. John le Carré, *A Small Town in Germany* (New York: Pocket Books, 2002), 298.

14. Ibid.

7. PRESENTATION

1. Jacob Nielsen's Alertbox, September 12, 2011.

2. Fred A. Bernstein, "Architecture Firm Websites: The Good, the Bad, the Ugly," *Architectural Record*, June 25, 2012.

A former architecture critic for *New York* magazine, **CARTER WISEMAN** teaches history and writing at the Yale School of Architecture. He is the author of *I. M. Pei: A Profile in American Architecture; Twentieth-Century American Architecture: The Buildings and Their Makers;* and *Louis I. Kahn: Beyond Time and Style.* A graduate of Yale College, Wiseman received a master's degree in architectural history from Columbia University and was a Loeb Fellow in Advanced Environmental Studies at the Harvard University Graduate School of Design. He is a past president of the MacDowell Colony, the nation's oldest retreat for creative artists.